Learn Chinese Characters 1

Chan Kwok Kin and William
(With the assistance of Pauline Ng L

Third Edition

Greenwood Press

GREENWOOD PRESS
47 Pokfulam Road, Basement, Hong Kong.
Telephone: 2546 8212

© *Greenwood Press 1992, 1993, 1996*
All rights reserved. No part of this publication may be reproduced, stored in a retrieval system, or transmitted in any form or by any means – electronic, mechanical, photo-copying, or otherwise – without the prior permission of the copyright owner.

First Edition 1992
Second Edition 1993
Third Edition 1996
    Reprinted 2000.

ISBN 962-279-176-X

PRINTED IN HONG KONG

Contents

1. Preface to the Third Edition 1
2. Introduction 2
3. Guide to Pronunciation 6
4. General List of Key Characters 12
5. 120 Key Characters 21
6. Numbers 142
7. Numbers on Minibus and Market Price Signs 143
8. Major Buildings 145
9. Hotels 148
10. Major Hospitals 153
11. Major Banks 155
12. Streets and Roads
    Hong Kong Island 157
    Kowloon 161
13. MTR Stations 164
14. KCR Stations 167
15. Cinemas, Theatres and Cultural Venues 168
16. Tourist and Sightseeing Places 171
17. Some Common Surnames 175
18. Some Chinese Restaurants 179

Preface to the Third Edition

Launched in 1992, this little practical book has clearly filled a need and 1993 saw the second edition, with a general updating of the names of the hotels, buildings, places of entertainment and photos. Now, in 1996, the second edition is sold out and we are faced with the need for a new edition with further revisions to keep pace with the dynamic changes in Hong Kong. This time we have decided to do a much more extensive revision. The number of key characters has now been increased from 104 to 120. Several of the new characters have to do with prohibition (**mat**_ 'don't', **jee**ˊ 'stop', **jeun**ˊ 'permit', **fong**ˋ 'prevent', **gam**‾ 'prohibit'). This is not perhaps surprising given that public notices are frequently concerned with regulating behaviour. Two new directions have been included (**dung**ˋ 'east', **bak**‾ 'north') as well as **tung**ˋ 'pass through', all of which may be found on place names or traffic signs. There are also some useful new additions like **neuy**ˊ 'woman', **meen**_ 'noodles' and **seung**ˋ 'business'.

Other changes have included once again a general revision of the places, names and photos. In view of the expected changes in the names of government departments from 1997 this section has been dropped for the present edition but will be restored in future editions. Again, as the simplified characters in use in Mainland China are expected to become more common, their importance has been enhanced by placing them at the top nearer to the unsimplified key characters currently in use in Hong Kong. These and other changes have been made so that the end product will be as useful for the late 90s as its predecessors were for the early and mid-90s. We are confident that there will be a fourth edition in the not-too-distant future.

Chan Kwok Kin & William Crewe   Hong Kong, 1996

Introduction

This book has arisen from the collaboration of a Cantonese language learner and a Cantonese language teacher. In this way we hope to obtain the best of both worlds: accuracy plus utility. The learner was able to advise on what aspects of the Chinese script would be interesting and useful, how much would constitute digestible morsels and what would give immediate returns for the effort expended; the teacher was able to translate these requirements into linguistic reality.

The book concentrates on the visible, public Chinese as seen on shops and buildings, street names, bus and MTR destinations, public signs and notices, and other places the average person walking or riding around Hong Kong and Kowloon will encounter every day. (Occasionally, where an important or useful character was not represented by a wide range of public displays we have turned to menus or retail products to supply examples.) By recognising and understanding these names, the casual visitor to Hong Kong will gain a valuable insight into the structure of Chinese words while the learner of Chinese will gain the kind of reinforcement necessary to aid memorisation with the minimum of effort.

The book is aimed, then, at two kinds of reader: one is **the tourist, the visitor, the non-specialist in Chinese.** For him/her we have tried to make the pronunciation system as simple as is consistent with accuracy and we have made the learning/recognition load associated with each character not too weighty (only 4 sample uses per character). The other kind of reader is **the beginning learner of Cantonese.** Not only have we been extra careful about the accuracy of our transcriptions but for him/her we have supplied three additional systems to give ease of linkage with whatever system they are using to learn. The basic system employed is a modified Yale system (modified by, for example, removing the low-register **h** symbol and changing some of the other less immediate representations of sounds like **yu** to **ü**). But because it may be irksome for those people studying through the original Yale system to mentally adjust the transcription we have supplied this in full at the bottom of each page. Books using the increasingly popular Yale system include *Everyday Cantonese, Basic Cantonese in 100 Hours, Speak Cantonese* and all the materials produced by the Chinese University and Hong Kong University Language Learning Centres. Another common system is that used by Sidney Lau in *Elementary Cantonese, Intermediate Cantonese,* etc and it is used in *Getting Around in Hong Kong*. We have included transcriptions in this system in order to make the book accessible to learners using these (older) books too. Finally, in case the book should also be of interest to people learning or already possessing a knowledge of Mandarin (Putonghua) we have included the Pinyin system and the simplified characters. It should be noted, however, that the Pinyin examples offered are merely *Cantonese words in Mandarin pronunciation:* sometimes the words are indeed the true Mandarin words but at other times, e.g. with words like 'bus' and 'taxi' quite different words are used in China. (It would make little sense to give the actual Mandarin words instead, as the corresponding characters would also be different and not in use in Hong Kong.)

At the end of the book we have included a list of commonly used names of hotels, streets, districts, cinemas, hospitals, buildings, etc to aid the traveller *and* the resident. The key feature here is the pronunciation guide so that one can actually *tell* the taxi driver rather than having to *show* him the characters in the back of the Street Guide. Unfortunately, because of restrictions on space we are unable to include the full Yale, Lau and Pinyin systems here but as the basic system is intended to be easily accessible even to the non-specialist this should not be too much of a disadvantage.

The core of the book contains 120 Key Characters all of which are common and publicly visible in Hong Kong. These are combined with (usually) four other sets of characters to give compounds which are also publicly on display. Some of these are general terms like 'bank', 'centre' and 'bus'; others are specific place names like 'The Peak', 'Admiralty' and 'Star Ferry'. Both kinds of name are equally visible and it seems desirable to include such proper names in the examples because of their utility, as well as their visibility. In spite of their high value to the learner they are frequently missing from coursebooks and, if for nothing else, this book can be a valuable source of such names. Analysing the names (which are often more transparent in Chinese than in English) is a way of aiding understanding and memorisation both of the characters and of the pronunciation. So we have also supplied the meanings for all of the parts of the compound examples for greater clarity. With some of the compounds the other parts may feature as Key Characters in their own right and this kind of 'cross-referencing' will aid memorisation and recognition. Because, however, we can only include a random selection of proper names in the Key Character section we have given at the back, for the sake of comprehensiveness and ease of reference, lists of these and other useful names. These lists are selective and mainly devoted to the high-profile central districts of Hong Kong and Kowloon.

The Key Characters, apart from the standard numbers and market/minibus price card numbers, are *arranged in the order of the complexity of the word*, that is, the number of strokes used to make up the word. The number and order of writing the strokes are illustrated in the horizontal boxes. In order to find a word, simply count the number of strokes: the simplest Key Character is given at the beginning and has 2 strokes while the most complex comes at the end with 25 strokes. This is *one* of the systems used in Chinese dictionaries. (Unfortunately, in the commonest system you have to identify first the Radical part of the word and count the strokes in that part in order to locate it in the list of 214 Radicals, then count the strokes in the other part of the word and look it up according to the number of strokes in the list of words under the particular Radical. This is far too difficult for our purposes!)

Each Key Character page is complete in itself and the book as a whole is designed for browsing rather than for working through systematically – though, as it builds up in complexity, it is also possible to learn the characters in this sequence beginning with the simplest ones.

Sometimes there are alternative forms of the character in use in Hong Kong and these forms have been indicated. at the bottom right hand side of the page. We have also indicated the Simplified Characters in use for Mandarin beside the Key Character. Generally, these two additional forms are the same though very occasionally they differ (see Key Character 81).

A further point that needs explanation for the non-specialist is that spoken and written Cantonese do not always coincide: written Cantonese is much more formal and sometimes uses entirely different words from the colloquial, for example, in the expression of time where the written form for 'hour' is pronounced *see* but the spoken form is ***deem***. Where this is likely to lead the tourist/student into incomprehensibility we have indicated this difference.

The authors hope this book will supply an easy way into the complexities of Chinese characters and an understanding of their structure and meaning.

Guide to Pronunciation

| Consonants ||||
Initial	Final	Initial	Final
b		f	
d		h	
g		s	
p	p	j	
t	t	ch	
k	k	gw	
l		kw	
m	m	w	w
n	n	y	y
ng	ng		

All the consonants are pronounced approximately as in English, except

1) Final **p, t, k** are 'unreleased', that is to say, the lips (for **p**) and the tongue against the teeth (for **t**) and against the palate (for **k**) close but do not open again. The sound appears to be 'cut off' or 'clipped'.

2) Initial **ng** in, for example, **ngor** is like in English **'ring or knock'**. Try to remove the **ri** .....

knock, leaving only **ngor.** Notice, however, that initial **ng** can always be omitted so the word can also be pronounced as **or.**

3) Initial **s, j** and **ch** may sometimes be heard as **sh, dz** and **ts** respectively but this is just a variation and is not significant.

4) Initial **p, t, k** and **ch/ts** are also 'unreleased' (see above) and may often sound more like **b, d, g** and **j/dz** to the British or American ear.

5) Initial n may often be pronounced as **l** in colloquial speech (but notice that an original **l** should never be pronounced as **n**).

Short Vowels

a   as in English 'cat' (often like the vowel in 'cut')
i   as in English 'sit'
o   as in English 'lot'
u   as in English 'put' or 'bush'

Long Vowels

All the long vowels are **one sound,** not two sounds: <u>**aa**</u> not a-a.
aa   like the 'a' in 'bad' lengthened (*not* like the 'a' in 'bar')
e   as in English 'bed' but slightly lengthened
ee   as in English 'bee' (*not* like 'bed' lengthened)

	Pure Vowels		Diphthongs	
	Short	Long	Short	Long
	a	aa	ai	aay
			au	aaw
		e	ei	
	i	ee		
	o	or	ou	
			oi	
	u	oo		yu
				ooy
		eu		euy
		ü		

or   as in English 'or' (no 'r' sound)
oo   as in English 'moon' (*not* like 'hot' lengthened)
eu   as in English 'err' or 'learn' (no 'r' sound)
ü   as in 'German 'grün or French 'lune': pronounce 'i' with rounded lips.

Diphthongs

Diphthongs glide from one sound into the other: they are *not* two separate sounds.

ai   as in English 'bite'

aay as in English 'fly' only longer
au as in English 'out'
aaw as in English 'now' only longer
ei as in English 'date'
ou as in English 'note'
oi as in English 'hoist'
yu as in English 'you'
ooy as in English 'boo' + a 'y' sound at the end, in one long glide
euy as in English 'fur + a 'y' sound at the end, in one long glide
(there is no 'r' sound: French 'seuil' or 'feuille' is closer)

Note that **ai/aay** and **au/aaw** are essentially the same sound but the second one is longer. **ei, ou** and **oi** are short sounds and **yu, ooy** and **euy** are long sounds.

(The pronunciation of the Yale, Lau and Pinyin systems is not dealt with explicity in this book. They are included for learners who already know the systems.)

Tones

The tones are important in Cantonese especially in the pronunciation of *single* words. Words in combination may be more intelligible even with faulty tones. Cantonese has 7 tones (some systems, e.g. Lau, count 10 by treating the 'clipped tones' - the combination of final 'p', 't' and 'k' with low/mid/high level - as 3 separate tones). Also, as there is no distinction for most speakers between the high level and high falling tones, the absolute number of tones may even be reduced to 6. The tones are:

High level (5→5)	see⁻	poem
High falling (5→3)	see\	to tear
High rising (3→5)	see/	history
Mid level (3→3)	see⁻	to try
Low level (2→2)	see_	matter
Low falling (2→1)	see\	time
Low rising (1→2)	see/	market

They may be represented graphically as follows:

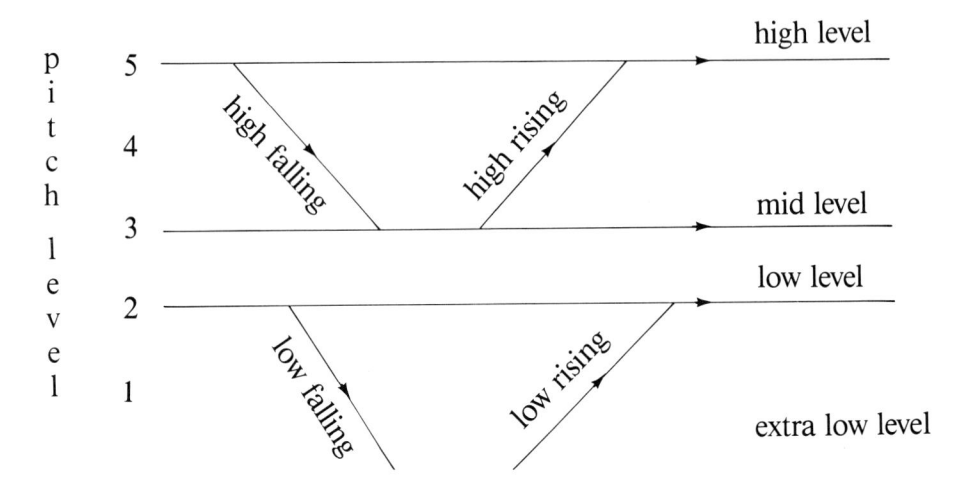

In marking the tones on the words we have adopted the simplest system possible - the height and direction of the mark exactly represent the pitch and movement of the voice, whether it is high, mid or low and whether it is falling or rising. There are no complicated numbers or symbols to remember.

General List of Key Characters

Two strokes
       Page

1)	人	yan`\`	man	22
2)	入	yap_	enter	23

Three strokes

3)	下	haa_	lower, under	24
4)	工	gung`\`	work	25
5)	士	see´; see_	the sound 'see' in foreign words	26
6)	大	daay	big	27
7)	口	hau´	mouth	28
8)	小	syu´	small	29
9)	山	saan`\`	mountain	30
10)	上	seung_ ; seung´	upper part, go up	31
11)	女	neuy´	female; daughter	32

Four strokes

12)	文	man`\`	language	33

13)	元	yün﹨	dollar	34
14)	天	teen﹨	sky	35
15)	不	bat―	not	36
16)	太	taay―	eldest son in the royal family; supreme	37
17)	日	yat_	day	38
18)	中	jung﹨	middle	39
19)	水	seuy╱	water	40
20)	牛	ngau﹨	cow	41
21)	午	ng╱	a session of the day; noon	42
22)	分	fan﹨	branch; divide; minute	43
23)	公	gung﹨	public	44
24)	手	sau╱	hand	45
25)	心	sam﹨	heart	46
26)	火	for╱	fire	47
27)	巴	baa―	the sound 'ba' in foreign words	48
28)	止	jee╱	stop; end	49
29)	勿	mat_	don't	50

Five strokes

30)	市	see╱	market, city	51
31)	半	boon―	half	52

13

32)	田	teenˋ	rice field	53
33)	出	cheut⁻	go out	54
34)	仔	jai´	suffix for 'small'	55
35)	北	bak⁻	north	56
36)	台(臺)	toiˋ	platform; station; terrace	57

Six strokes

37)	百	baak⁻	hundred	58
38)	西	saiˋ	west	59
39)	地	dei⁻	ground	60
40)	行	hangˋ; hong´; hongˋ	walk, firm	61
41)	年	neenˋ	year	62

Seven strokes

42)	沙	saaˋ	sand	63
43)	車	cheˋ	vehicle	64
44)	折	jeet⁻	discount	65
45)	邨(村)	chün⁻	estate	66
46)	局	guk⁻ ; guk´	council, establishment	67
47)	門	moonˋ	door	68

14

48)	角	gok⁻	point of land	69
49)	防	fongˋ	prevent	70

Eight strokes

50)	店	deem⁻	shop	71
51)	花	faaˋ	flower	72
52)	亞	aa⁻	the sound 'aa' in foreign words	73
53)	具	geui_	object, item	74
54)	往	wong´	to (toward)	75
55)	金	gam⁻	gold	76
56)	季	gwai⁻	season	77
57)	東	dungˋ	east	78

Nine strokes

58)	音	yamˋ	audio; sound	79
59)	美	mei´	beautiful	80
60)	洲	jauˋ	continent	81
61)	洗	sai´	wash	82
62)	室	sat⁻	room	83
63)	城	singˋ	city	84

64)	星	sing`	star	85
65)	品	ban´	article, thing	86
66)	香	heung`	fragrant	87
67)	界	gaay–	side; boundary	88

Ten strokes

68)	家	gaa`	family	89
69)	酒	jau´	wine	90
70)	海	hoi´	sea	91
71)	座	jor–	housing block; seat (in theatre)	92
72)	高	gou`	high	93
73)	站	jaam–	station, stop	94
74)	茶	chaa`	tea	95
75)	時	see`	hour	96
76)	島 (岛)	dou´	island	97
77)	租	jou`	rent	98
78)	院	yün´	a courtyard	99
79)	准	jeun´	permit	100

Eleven strokes

| 80) | 部 | bou– | department | 101 |

81)	厠(廁)	chee–	toilet, lavatory	102
82)	票	pyu–	ticket	103
83)	區	keuy˴	district	104
84)	國	gwok–	country	105
85)	處	chü–	place	106
86)	售	sau˗	sell	107
87)	停	ting˴	stop	108
88)	通	tung˴	pass through	109
89)	商	seung˴	trade; business	110

Twelve strokes

90)	菜	choi–	dish of food; cuisine; vegetable	111
91)	場(塲)	cheung˴	spacious area	112
92)	港	gong˴	harbour	113
93)	街	gaay–	street	114
94)	等	dang˴	wait	115

Thirteen strokes

95)	新	san˴	new	116
96)	道	dou˗	road	117

17

97)	電	deen⁻	electricty	118
98)	號	hou⁻	number	119
99)	業	yeep⁻	trade	120
100)	園	yün´	leisure place	121
101)	裝	jong⁻	wear, style	122
102)	會	wooy´; wooy⁻	meeting; association	123
103)	飾	sik⁻	decoration	124
104)	禁	gam⁻	prohibit	125
105)	傳	chün˴	pass; call; spread	126

Fourteen strokes

106)	碼	maa⁄	ferry pier	127
107)	樓	lau˴	building	128
108)	銀	ngan˴	silver	129

Fifteen strokes

109)	請	ching´	please	130
110)	賣	maay⁻	sell	131
111)	價	gaa⁻	price	132

Sixteen strokes

112)	機	gei`	machine	133
113)	學	hok_	learn	134
114)	險	heem´	risk; risky	135
115)	餐	chaan¯	meal	136
116)	館	goon´	building	137

Seventeen strokes

| 117) | 龍 | lung` | dragon | 138 |

Eighteen strokes

| 118) | 醫 | yee` | cure | 139 |

Twenty strokes

| 119) | 麵(麺) | meen_ | noodle | 140 |

Twenty five strokes

| 120) | 灣 | waan¯ | bay | 141 |

120 Key Characters

| 人 | Yan＼ | man |

| ノ 人 |

行人	hang＼ (walk)	yan＼ man)			pedestrian
成人	sing＼ (change to)	yan＼ man)			adult (e.g. on MTR adult tickets)
華人銀行	Waa＼ (Chinese)	yan＼ man	Ngan＼ silver	hong＼ firm)	Hong Kong Chinese Bank
閒人免進	haan＼ (leissure)	yan＼ man	meen／ don't	jeun— enter)	No trespassing

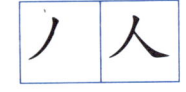

Yale System : yàhn, hàhngyàhn, sìhngyàhn, Wàhyàhn Ngàhnhòhng, hàahn yàhn míhn jeun

Lau System : yan⁴, hang⁴ yan⁴, sing⁴ yan⁴, Wa⁴ yan⁴ Ngan⁴ hong⁴, haan⁴ yan⁴ min⁵ jun³

Pinyin : rén, xíngrén, chéngrén, Huárén Yínháng, xián rén miǎn jìn

入

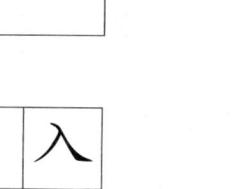

Yapˍ   enter

| ノ | 入 |

入口	yapˍ (enter)	hau´ mouth)		entrance
入場	yapˍ (enter)	cheungˎ spacious area)		entrance (theatre, cinema, etc.)
不准駛入	bat¯ (not)	jeun´ permit	sai´ drive	yapˍ enter)	Do not drive in (traffic signs placed at road entrance)
不准進入	bat¯ (not)	jeun´ permit	jeun— advance	yapˍ enter)	Do not enter

Yale System : yahp, yahpha
ú, yahpchèuhng, bātjeún sáiyahp, bātjeún jeunyahp
Lau System   : yap⁶, yap⁶ hau², yap⁶ cheung⁴, bat¹⁰ jun² sai² yap⁶, bat¹⁰ jun² jun³ yap⁶
Pinyin   : rù, rùkǒu, rùchǎng, bùzhǔn shǐrù, bùzhǔn jìnrù

23

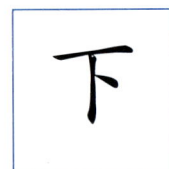

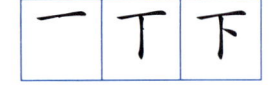

下　　Haa ˍ , Haa ´　　lower, under

一丁下

下午	haa ˍ (lower	ng ∕ noon)		afternoon
地下	dei ˍ (ground	haa ˍ (haa ´) under)		ground floor
下午茶	haa ˍ (lower	ng ∕ noon	chaa ˎ tea)	afternoon tea
地下鐵路	Dei ˍ (ground	haa ˍ under	Teet ˉ　lou ˍ iron　　road)	Mass Transit Railway (often referred to as dei ˍ teet ˉ in speaking)

Yale System : hah, hahngh, deihhah, hahngh chàh, Deihhah Titlouh

Lau System : ha⁶, ha⁶ ng⁵, dei⁶ ha⁶, ha⁶ ng⁵ cha⁴, Dei⁶ ha⁶ Tit³ lo⁶

Pinyin : xià, xiàwǔ, dìxià, xiàwǔ chá, Dìxià Tiělù

| 工 | Gungˋ | work |

| 一 | 丁 | 工 |

工人	gungˋ (work)	yanˍ (person)	worker
工廠 (厰)	gungˋ (work)	chong´ (factory)	factory
工業	gungˋ (work)	yeepˍ (trade)	industry
工會	gungˋ (work)	wooy´ (association)	trade union
水電工程	seuy´ (water)	deenˍ (electric) gungˋ chingˋ (engineering)	pump and electric appliances repair

Yale System : gùng, gùngyàhn, gùngchóng, gùngyihp, gùngwúi, séui dihn gùng chìhng

Lau System : gung¹, gung¹ yan⁴, gung¹ chong², gung¹ yip⁶, gung¹ wooi², sui² din⁶ gung¹ ching⁴

Pinyin : gōng, gōngrén, gōngchǎng, gōngyè, gōnghuì, shuǐ diàn gōngchéng

25

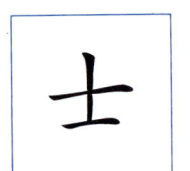

士 See´, See_   the sound 'see' in foreign words

一 十 士

士多	see_ dor¯	store (corner shops often named 士多)
巴士	baa¯ see´	bus
的士	dik¯ see´	taxi
勞力士	Lou` lik_ see´	Rolex

Yale System : sí, sihdō, bāsí, dīksí, Lòuhlihksí
Lau System : si², si⁶ doh¹⁰, ba¹⁰ si², dik¹⁰ si², Lo⁴ lik⁶ si²
Pinyin : shì, shìduō, bāshì, dìshì, Láolìshì

26

大

Daay_ big

一 ナ 大

大丸	Daay_	yün/		Daimaru (a Japanese department store in Causeway Bay)
大堂	daay_ (big	tong\ hall)		lobby, foyer
大廈	daay_ (big	haa_ building)		high-rise building (name of commercial buildings often end in this)
大減價	daay_ (big	gaam/ reduce	gaa– price)	big sale
黄大仙	Wong\ (Wong[surname]	daay_ big	seen\ fairy)	Wong Tai Sin (MTR stop, also famous temple)

Yale System : daaih, Daaihyún, daaihtòhng, daaihhah, daaih gáamga, Wòhngdaaihsìn

Lau System : daai^{6}, Daai^{6} yuen^{2}, daai^{6} tong^{4}, daai^{6} ha^{6}, daai^{6} gaam^{2} ga^{3}, Wong^{4} daai^{6} sin^{1}

Pinyin : dà, Dàwán, dàtáng, dàshà, dà jiănjià, Huángdàxiān

Haú   mouth

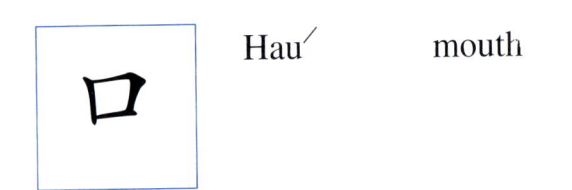

入口	yap_ (enter)	haú (mouth)	entrance/import
出口	cheut⁻ (go out)	haú (mouth)	exit/export
出入口	cheut⁻ (go out)	yap_ (enter)	haú (mouth)	import/export (company)/exit and entrance
隧道口	seuy_ (hollow)	dou_ (road)	haú (mouth)	tunnel entrance

Yale System : háu, yahpháu, chēutháu, chēutyahpháu, seuihdouh háu

Lau System : hau², yap⁶ hau², chut¹⁰ hau², chut¹⁰ yap⁶ hau², sui⁶ do⁶ hau²

Pinyin : kǒu, rùkǒu, chūkǒu, chùrùkǒu, suìdào kǒu

小 Syu´ small

丿 小 小

小心	syu´ (small)	sam` (heart)	careful; danger! (on public signs)
小學	syu´ (small)	hok_ (study)	primary school
小食	syu´ (small)	sik_ (eat)	snack (on menu)
小童	syu´ (small)	tung` (boy)	children (e.g. fare sign)

Yale System : síu, síusàm, síuhohk, síusihk, síutùhng
Lau System : siu², siu² sam¹, siu² hok⁶, siu² sik⁶, siu² tung⁴
Pinyin : xiǎo, xiǎoxīn, xiǎoxué, xiǎoshí, xiǎotóng

| 山 |

Saan`   mountain

| 丨 | 山 | 山 |

山頂	Saan` (mountain)	deng´ top)		The Peak
半山	Boon– (half)	saan` mountain)		Mid-levels
大嶼山	Daay– (big)	yü´ island	Saan` mountain)	Lantau Island
歷山大廈	Lik– (Alexandra	saan`	Daay– big	haa– building)	Alexandra House (in Central)

Yale System   :   sàan, Sàandéng, Bunsàan, Daaihyùh Sàan, Lihksàan Daaihhah

Lau System   :   saan¹, Saan¹ deng², Boon³ saan¹ Daai⁶ yue⁴ Saan¹, Lik⁶ saan¹ Daai⁶ ha⁶

Pinyin   :   shān, Shāndǐng, Bànshān, Dàyǔ Shān, Lìshān Dàshà

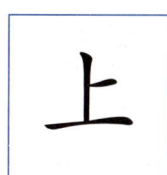

上	Seung˗ ; upper part
	seung╱ go up

一	卜	上

早上	jou╱ (early)	seung˗ upper)	morning
晚上	maan╱ (night)	seung˗ upper)	evening
上門	seung╱ (go up)	moon╱ door)	door to door (shop service sign)
上車	seung╱ (go up)	che╲ car)	board a car
上午	seung˗ (upper)	ng╱ noon)	morning

Yale System : seuhng, jóuseuhng, máahnseuhng, séuhngmún, séuhng chè, seuhng ńgh

Lau System : seung⁶, jo² seung⁶, maan⁵ seung⁶, seung⁵ moon², seung⁵ che¹, seung⁶ ng⁵

Pinyin : shàng, zǎoshang, wǎnshang, shàngmén, shàngchē, shàngwǔ

31

女   Neuy╱   female; daughter

女厸女 **FEMALE TOILET**

女界	neuy╱ (female)	gaay— side)			lady's restroom
女賓	neuy╱ (female)	ban╲ guest)			female customer
婦女	foo╱ (wife)	neuy╱ female)			women
女青年會	Neuy╱ (female	Ching╲ young	neen╲ year	Wooy╱ association)	Y. W. C. A.

Yale System : néuih, néuih gaai, néuih bàn, fúhnéuih, Néuih Chìngnìhn Wúi

Lau System : nui[5], nui[5] gaai[3], nui[5] ban[1], foo[5] nui[5], Nui[5] Ching[1] nin[4] Wooi[2]

Pinyin : nǚ, nǚ jiè, nü bīn, fùnǚ, Nǚ Qīngnián Huì

文   Màn language
     Man´ (rising tone, often used in speaking)

**HONG KONG CULTURAL C
CONCERT HALL 8 PM
香港文化中心音樂廳**

丶　一　亠　文

文化中心	Màn (language)	faa– culture	Jùng centre	sàm heart)	Cultural Centre
中文	Jùng (middle)	man (man´) language)			Chinese
英文	Yìng	man (man´) (language)			English
法文	Faat–	man (man´) (language)			French
德文	Dāk–	man (man´) (language)			German

Yale System   : màhn, Màhnfa Jùngsàm, Jùngmàhn, Yìngmàhn, Faatmàhn, Dākmàhn

Lau System   : man⁴, Man⁴ fa³ Jung¹ sam¹, Jung¹ man⁴, Ying¹ man⁴, Faat³ man⁴, Dak¹⁰ man⁴

Pinyin   : wén, Wénhuà Zhōngxīn, Zhōngwén, Yīngwén, Fǎwén, Déwén

| 元 | Yünˋ dollar (spoken form man¯) |

| 一 | 二 | 亍 | 元 |

五元　　ng／　　yünˋ　　　　　　　　　　　five dollars (spoken: ng／ man¯)
　　　　(five) (dollar)

美元　　Mei／　yünˋ　　　　　　　　　　　U.S. dollar
　　　　(America) (dollar)

港元　　Gong／　yünˋ　　　　　　　　　　H.K. dollar
　　　　(Hong Kong) (dollar)

罰款 1,000元　fat_　　foon／　yat¯　cheenˋ　yünˋ　penalty $1,000
　　　　　　(　penalty　　　one　thousand　dollars)　(inside MTR train compartments)

Yale System　:　yùhn, ńghyùhn, Méihyùhn, Góngyùhn, fahtfún yātchìn yùhn

Lau System　:　yuen⁴, ng⁵ yuen⁴, Mei⁵ yuen⁴, Gong² yuen⁴, fat⁶ foon² yat¹⁰ chin¹ yuen⁴

Pinyin　　　:　yuán, wǔyuán, Měiyuán, Gǎngyuán, fákuǎn yìqiān yuán

| 天 |

Teen` sky

| 一 | 二 | 干 | 天 |

天后廟	Teen` (sky)	hau‾ (queen)	Meeu´ temple)	Temple of Goddess of the Sea (Tin Hau is an MTR stop on the HK line)
天星小輪	Teen` (sky)	sing` star	Syu´ small	leun` ferry)	Star Ferry
通天巴士	Tung` (go through)	teen` sky	Baa‾ bus)	see´	Airbus
天橋	teen` (sky)	kyu´ bridge)			flyover, footbridge

Yale System : tìn, Tìnhauh Míu, Tìnsìng Síulèuhn, Tùngtìn Bāsí, tìnkìuh

Lau System : tin[1], Tin[1] hau[6] Miu[2], Tin[1] sing[1] Siu[2] lun[4], Tung[1] tin[1] Ba[10] si[2], tin[1] kiu[4]

Pinyin : tiàn, Tiānhòu Miào, Tiānxīng Xiǎolún, Tōngtiān Bāshì, tiānqiáo

35

不   Bat⁻   not
(on public signs)

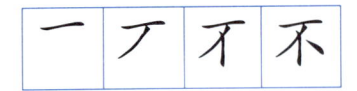

一 丁 不 不

不便	bat⁻ (not)	been₋ convenient)			inconvenient (on road-up sign)
不准	bat⁻ (not)	jeun╱ permit)			not permitted
不可	bat⁻ (not)	hor╱ can)			cannot
不准吸煙	bat⁻ (not)	jeun╱ permit	kap⁻ inhale	yeen⁻ smoke)	No smoking

Yale System : bāt, bātbihn, bātjéun, bāthó, bātjéun kāpyīn
Lau System : bat¹⁰, bat¹⁰ bin⁶, bat¹⁰ jun², bat¹⁰ ho², bat¹⁰ jun² kap¹⁰ yin¹⁰
Pinyin : bù, bùbiàn, bùzhǔn, bùkě, bùzhǔn xīyān

| 太 | Taay– | eldest son in the royal family; supreme |

一 ナ 大 太

太陽眼鏡	taay– (sun	yeung＼	ngaan／ ngaan glasses)	geng–	sunglasses
太古城	Taay– (supreme	gwoo／ ancient	sing＼ city)		Tai Koo Shing (MTR Stop)
太空館	Taay– (supreme	hung＼ vacant	Gwoon／ hall)		Space Museum (in Tsimshatsui)
太古大廈	Taay– (supreme	gwoo／ ancient	Daay– big	haa– building)	Swire House (in Central)

Yale System : taai, taaiyèuhng ngáahngeng, Taaigwú Sìhng, Taaihùng Gwún, Taaigwú Daaihhah

Lau System : taai³, taai³ yeung⁴ ngaan⁵ geng³, Taai³ gwu² Sing⁴, Taai³ hung¹ Gwun², Taai³ gwu² Daai⁶ ha⁶

Pinyin : tài, táiyang yǎnjìng, Tàigǔ Chéng, Tàikong Guǎn, Tàigǔ Dàshà

| 日 | Yat‾ day |

| 丨 | 冂 | 日 | 日 |

日本	Yat‾	boon´		Japan
全日	chün` (whole)	yat‾ (day)		whole day (road sign)
即日	jik‾ (instant)	yat‾ (day)		today (cinema sign)
星期日	Sing` (star)	kei´ (period)	yat‾ (day)	Sunday

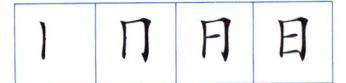

Yale System : yaht, Yahtbún, chyùhnyaht, jīkyaht, Sìngkèihyaht
Lau System : yat⁶, Yat⁶ boon², chuen⁴ yat⁶, jik¹⁰ yat⁶, Sing¹ kei⁴ yat⁶
Pinyin : rì, Rìběn, quánrì, jírì, Xīngqīrì

| 中 | Jungˋ | middle |

| 丶 | 冂 | 口 | 中 |

中心	jungˋ (middle)	samˋ heart)	centre
中國	Jungˋ (Middle)	gwok⁻ Kingdom)	China
中環	Jungˋ (middle)	waanˋ enclose)	Central District
中文大學	Jungˋ (Chinese	manˋ language	Daay⁻ hok⁻ University)	The Chinese University of Hong Kong

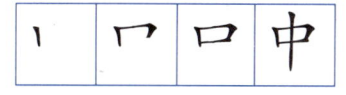

Yale System : jùng, jùngsàm, Jùnggwok, Jùngwàahn, Jùngmàhn Daaihhohk

Lau System : jung¹, jung¹ sam¹, Jung¹ gwok³, Jung¹ waan⁴, Jung¹ man⁴ Daai⁶ hok⁶

Pinyin : zhōng, Zhōngxīn, Zhōngguó, Zhōnghuán, Zhōngwén Dàxúe

| 水 | Seuy´ | water |

| 亅 | 刀 | 水 | 水 |

WATER SUPPLIES DEPARTMENT
水務署

水警	seuy´ (water)	ging´ (police)	marine police
汽水	hei— (bubble)	seuy´ (water)	softdrink
風水	fung` (wind)	seuy´ (water)	Fung Shui (Chinese superstition)
水上樂園	Seuy´ (water)	seung— (on top)	Lok— (happy)	yün` (garden)	Water World (in Ocean Park)
淺水灣	Cheen´ (shallow)	seuy´ (water)	Waan— (bay)	Repulse Bay

Yale System : séui, séui gíng, heiséui, fūngséui, Séuiseuhng Lohkyùhn, Chínséui Wāan

Lau System : sui^2, sui^2 ging^2, hei^3 sui^2, fung^1 sui^2, Sui^2 seung^6 Lok^6 yuen^4, Chin^2 sui^2 Waan^{10}

Pinyin : shuǐ, shuǐ jǐng, qìshuǐ, fēngshuǐ, shuǐshàng Lèyuán, Qían Shuǐ Wān

牛	Ngau ˋ	cow (on food store signs & restaurant menus)

丿 𠂉 𠄌 牛

牛扒	ngau ˋ paa ˊ (cow) (steak)	beef steak
牛肉	ngau ˋ yuk ˉ (cow) (meat)	beef
牛油	ngau ˋ yau ˊ (cow) (fat)	butter
牛奶公司	Ngau ˋ naay ˊ Gung ˋ see ˉ (cow) (milk) (public) (administration)	Dairy Farm Company

Yale System : ngàuh, ngàuh pá, ngàuhyuhk, ngàuhyàuh, Ngàuhnáaih gùngsī

Lau System : ngau[4], ngau[4] pa[2], ngau[4] yuk[6], ngau[4] yau[4], Ngau[4] naai[5] Gung[1] si[10]

Pinyin : niú, niúpái, niúròu, niúyóu, Niúnǎi Gōngsī

午   Ng╱   a session of the day, noon

丿 ㇒ 㐅 午

上午	seung‿ng╱ (upper noon)	morning (shop/business sign)
下午	haa‿ng╱ (lower noon)	afternoon (shop/business sign)
中午	jungˋ ng╱ (middle noon)	noon (shop/business sign)
午市	ng╱ see╱ (noon market)	lunch time business (restaurant sign)

Yale System : ńgh, seuhngńgh, hahńgh, jùngńgh, ńghsíh
Lau System : ng⁵, seung⁶ ng⁵, ha⁶ ng⁵, jung¹ ng⁵, ng⁵ si⁵
Pinyin : wǔ, shàngwǔ, xiàwǔ, zhōngwǔ, wǔshì

| 分 | Fanˋ | branch; divide; minute |

| 丿 | 八 | 分 | 分 |

分行	fanˋ (branch)	hong´ (company)	branch company
分店	fanˋ (branch)	deem– (shop)	branch shop
分期	fanˋ (divide)	kei´ (period)	by installment (shop signs)
四分半鐘	sei– (four | fanˋ minute | bun– half | jung– of clock)	four and a half minutes (seen at tram stations)

Yale System : fàn, fàn hóng, fàn dim, fàn kèih, seì fàn bun jūng
Lau System : fan[1], fan[1] hong[2], fan[1] dim[3], fan[1] kei[4], sei[3] fan[1] boon[3] jung[10]
Pinyin : fēn, fēn háng, fēn diàn, fēn qī, sìfēnbànzhōng

公　　Gung`　public

PUBLIC TOILET 公厠

| ノ | 八 | 公 | 公 |

公司	gung` (public)	see⁻ take charge of)	company, department store
公厠(廁)	gung` (public)	chee⁻ toilet)	public toilet
公眾	gung` (public)	jung⁻ mass)	General Public
辦公時間	baan⁻ (carry out | gung` public | see` time | gaan⁻ space)	office hours (shop/office sign)

Yale System : gùng, gùngsī, gùngchi, gùngjung, baahngùng sìhgaan

Lau System : gung¹, gung¹ si¹⁰, gung¹ chi³, gung¹ jung³, baan⁶ gung¹ si⁴ gaan³

Pinyin : gōng, gōngsī, gōngcè, gōngzhòng, bàngōng shíjiān

手 Sau′ hand

一 二 三 手

洗手間 LAVATORY

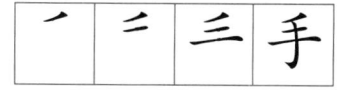

手袋	sau′ (hand)	doi′ (pocket)			handbag
二手車	yee_ (two)	sau′ (hand)	che﹨ (car)		second-hand car
緊握扶手	gan′ (tight)	aak⁻ (grasp)	foo﹨ (support)	sau′ (hand)	Hold the handrail (at esculators)
洗手間	sai′ (wash)	sau′ (hand)	gaan⁻ (area)		washroom

Yale System : sáu, sáudói, yihsáu chè, gánaāk fùhsáu, sáisáugaān

Lau System : sau², sau² doi², yi⁶ sau² che¹, gan² aak¹⁰ fu⁴ sau², sai² sau² gaan¹⁰

Pinyin : shǒu, shǒudài, èrshǒu chē, jǐng wò fúshǒu, xǐshǒujiān

45

心　　Samˋ　　heart

丶　心　心　心

中心	jungˋ (centre)	samˋ (heart)	centre (e.g. shopping centre)
小心	syu´ (small)	samˋ (heart)	be careful!; danger!
美心	Mei´	samˋ (heart)	Maxim's (a bakery/restaurant chain)
點心	deem´ (a little)	samˋ (heart)	dimsum (on menu)

Yale System : sàm, jùngsàm, síusàm, Méihsàm, dímsàm

Lau System : sam¹, jung¹ sam¹, siu² sam¹, Mei⁵ sam¹, dim² sam¹

Pinyin : xīn, zhōngxīn, xiǎoxīn, Měixīn, diǎnxīn

| 火 | | For´ | fire | |

| 、 | ノ | ㄎ | 火 |

火鍋	for´ (fire	wor` pot)		hot pot (shop sign, also on menu)
火警	for´ (fire	ging´ alert)		fire alarm
防火	fong` (prevent	for´ fire)		fire precaution
滅火喉	meet_ (extinguish	for´ fire	hau` pipe)	fire hose

WHEN THERE IS A FIRE DO NOT USE THE LIFT

Yale System : fó, fówò, fógíng, fòhngfó, mihtfóhàuh

Lau System : foh², foh² woh¹, foh² ging², fong⁴ foh², mit⁶ foh² hau⁴

Pinyin : huǒ, huǒguō, huǒgǐng, fánghuǒ, mièhuǒhóu

巴　　Baa⁻　　the sound 'ba' in foreign words

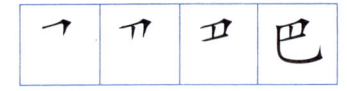

｜ ㄱ ㄲ 巴

巴士	baa⁻ (bus)	see´)			Bus
專線小巴	jyün` (special)	seen⁻ route	syu´ small	baa⁻ bus)	Maxi Cab
中巴	Jung` (China)	Baa⁻ bus)			China Motor Bus Company
九巴	Gau´ (Kowloon)	Baa⁻ bus)			Kowloon Motor Bus Company
城巴	Sing` (city)	Baa⁻ bus)			City Bus

Yale System : bā, bāsí, jyùnsin síubā, Jùng Bā, Gáu Bā, Sìhng Bā

Lau System : ba¹⁰, ba¹⁰ si², juen¹ sin³ siu² ba¹⁰, Jung¹ ba¹⁰, Gau² ba¹⁰ Sing⁴ Ba¹⁰

Pinyin　　　: bā, bāshì, zhuānxiàn xiǎobā, Zhōng Bā, Jiǔ Bā, Chéng Bā

止　　Jeeˊ　　　Stop; End

TUNNEL AREA END 隧道區域終止

| 丨 | 卜 | 止 | 止 |

行人止步　Hangˎ　yanˎ　jeeˊ　bou˗　No Trespassing
　　　　　(walk)　(person)　(stop)　(step)

停止　　　Tingˎ　jeeˊ　　　　　　　Stop
　　　　　(halt)　(stop)

禁止駛入　Gam˗　jiˊ　saiˊ　yap˗　No entry (traffic sign)
　　　　　(prohibit)　(stop)　(drive)　(enter)

禁止飲食　Gam˗　jiˊ　yamˊ　sik˗　No drinking, no eating
　　　　　(prohibit)　(stop)　(drink)　(eat)

Yale System : jí, Hàhngyàhn jí bouh, tìhngjí, Gamjí sái yahp, Gámjí yám sihk

Lau System : ji², Hang⁴ yan⁴ ji² bo⁶, ting⁴ ji², Gam³ ji² sai² yap⁶, Gam³ ji² yam² sik⁶

Pinyin　　 : zhǐ, Xíngrén zhǐ bù, tíngzhǐ, Jìnzhǐ shǐ rù, Jìnzhǐ yǐn shí

勿 Mat‿   don't

請勿與司機談話	Chíng (please)	mat‿ don't	yǜ with	see¯ driver	gei¯	taam˴	waa‿ talk)	Please don't talk to the driver
請勿吐痰	Chíng (please)	mat‿ don't	tou¯	taam˴ spit)				Please don't spit
請勿吸煙	Chíng (please)	mat‿ don't	kap¯ inhale	yin¯ smoke)				Please don't smoke
非請勿進	Fei˴ (not	chíng please	mat‿ don't	jeun¯ enter)				No entrance

Yale System : maht, Chíng maht yúh sīgēi tàahṃwah, Chíng maht tou tàahm, Chíng maht kāp yīn, Fèi chíng maht jeun

Lau System : mat⁶, Ching² mat⁶ yue⁵ si¹⁰ gei¹⁰ taam⁴ wa⁶, Ching² mat⁶ to³ taam⁴, Ching² mat⁶ kap¹⁰ yin¹⁰, Fei¹ ching² mat⁶ jun³

Pinyin : wù, Chǐng wù yǔ sījī tánhuà, Chǐng wù tù tán, Chǐng wù xīyān, Fēi qǐng wù jìn

市 See╱ market, city

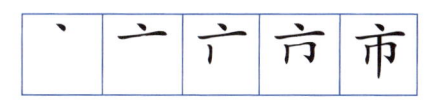

丶 亠 广 亣 市

市場	see╱ (market)	cheung╲ (spacious area)	market (clothing, etc)
市區	see╱ (city)	keuy╲ (district)	urban area (on road sign)
街市	gaay╲ (street)	see╱ (market)	market (food)
花市	faa╲ (flower)	see╱ (market)	flower market (at Chinese New Year)

Yale System   : sí, síhchèuhng, síhkeuì, gàaisíh, fàsíh
Lau System   : si[5], si[5] cheung[4], si[5] kui[1], gaai[1] si[5], fa[1] si[5]
Pinyin   : shì, shìchǎng, shìqū, jiēshì, huāshì

半

| 丶 | 丷 | 丷 | 半 | 半 |

半島酒店	Boon¯ (half	doúisland	Jaú deem¯ hotel)	Peninsula Hotel
半價	boon¯ (half	gaa¯ price)		half price (shop signs)
九時半	gaú (nine	see\ o'clock	boon¯ half)	half past nine (spoken: gaú deem´ boon¯)
半山區	Boon¯ (half	saan\ mountain	Keuy\ district)	Mid-levels

Yale System : bun, Bundóu Jáudim, bun ga, gáusìhbun, Bunsàan Keùi

Lau System : boon³, Boon do² Jau² dim³, Boon³ ga³, gau² si⁴ boon³, Boon³ saan¹ Kui¹

Pinyin : bàn, Bàndǎo Jiǔdìan, bànjià, jiǔshíbàn, Bànshānqū

| 田 |

Teen ↘ rice field

| 丨 | 冂 | 冂 | 冉 | 田 |

| 沙田 | Saa↘ (Sand) | teen↘ (rice-field) | Shatin (a new town in the New Territories, also a KCR train station) |

| 何文田 | Hor↘ | man↘ | teen↘ | Homantin (in Kowloon) |

| 本田 | Boon↗ | teen↘ | Honda (Japanese car) |

| 豐田 | Fung↘ | teen↘ | Toyota (Japanese car) |

Yale System   : tìhn, Sàtìhn, Hòhmàhntìhn, Búntìhn, Fùngtìhn

Lau System   : tin⁴, Sa¹ tin⁴, Hoh⁴ man⁴ tin⁴, Boon² tin⁴, Fung¹ tin⁴

Pinyin   : tián, Shātián, Héwéntián, Běntián, Fēngtián

53

出　　　Cheut⁻　　go out

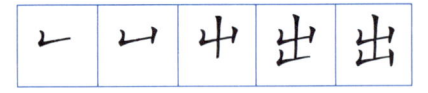

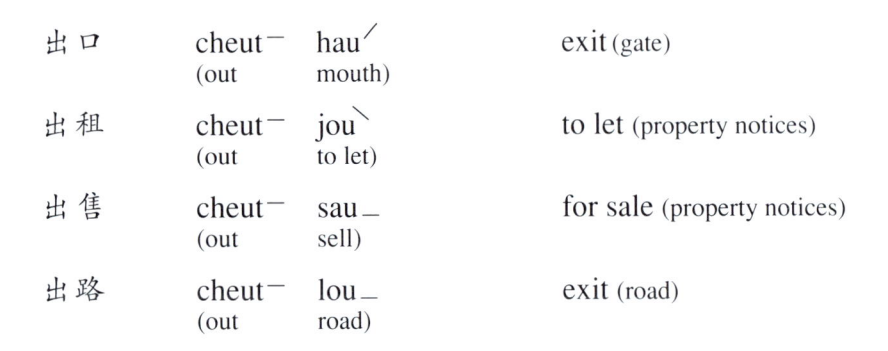

| 乚 | 凵 | 屮 | 出 | 出 |

出口　　cheut⁻　hau´　　　　exit (gate)
　　　　(out)　　(mouth)

出租　　cheut⁻　jou`　　　　to let (property notices)
　　　　(out)　　(to let)

出售　　cheut⁻　sau⁻　　　　for sale (property notices)
　　　　(out)　　(sell)

出路　　cheut⁻　lou⁻　　　　exit (road)
　　　　(out)　　(road)

Yale System　：　chēut, chēutháu, chēutjòu, chēutsauh, chēutlouh
Lau System　：　chut¹⁰, chut¹⁰ hau², chut¹⁰ jo¹, chut¹⁰ sau⁶, chut¹⁰ lo⁶
Pinyin　　　：　chū, chūkǒu, chūzū, chūshòu, chūlù

仔 　Jai´　　suffix for 'small'

ノ 　亻 　亻⸝ 　仔⸝ 　仔

灣仔	Waan⁻ (Bay)	jai´ (small)		Wan Chai
香港仔	Heung˴ (fragrant)	gong´ (harbour)	jai´ (small)	Aberdeen
氹仔	Tam ⁄ (waterhole)	jai´ (small)		Taipa (an island of Macau)

Yale System ：jái, Wāanjái, Hèunggóngjái, Táhmjái
Lau System ：jai², Waan¹⁰ jai², Heung¹ gong² jai², Tam⁵ jai²
Pinyin ：zǎi, Wānzǎi, Xiānggǎngzǎi, Dàngzǎi

55

Bak⁻　　north

北京　　Bak⁻　　ging`　　　Beijing
　　　　(north)　(capital)

北區　　Bak⁻　　keuy`　　　Northern District (in the New Territories)
　　　　(north)　(district)

北角　　Bak⁻　　gok⁻　　　North Point (district and MTR on HK Island).
　　　　(north)　(angle)

Yale System : bāk, Bākgìng, Bāk kèui, Bāk Gok

Lau System : bak¹⁰, Bak¹⁰ ging¹, Bak¹⁰ Kui¹, Bak¹⁰ gok³

Pinyin 　　　: běi, Běijīng, Běi Qū, Běijiǎo

台   Toiˎ   platform; station; terrace

| ㇄ | 厶 | 台 | 台 | 台 |

月台   Yüt‾   toiˎ   Platform (MTR, KCR)
         (moon) (platform)

電台   Din‾   toiˎ   Radio station
         (electric) (station)

電視台   Din‾   see‾   toiˎ   Television station
         (electric) (view) (station)

台灣   Toiˎ   waan‾   Taiwan (e.g. food shop)
         (platform) (bay)

炮台山   Paaw−   toiˎ   Saan˴   Fortress Hill (MTR station)
         (canon) (terrace) (mountain)

Yale System : tòih, yuhttòih, dihntòih, dihnsih tòih, Tòihwāan, Paautòih Sàan

Lau System : toi⁴, yuet⁶ toi⁴, din⁶ toi⁴, din⁶ si⁶ toi⁴, Toi⁴ waan¹⁰, Paau³ toi⁴ Saan¹

Pinyin   : tái, yuètái, diàntái, diànshì tái, Táiwān, Pàotái shān

臺

百　　Baakˉ　hundred

一　𠂉　丆　万　百　百

百佳	Baakˉ(hundred)	gaayˋ(good)			The Park'n Shop (a supermarket chain)
百貨公司	baakˉ(hundred)	for˗(commodity)	gungˋ(public)	seeˉ(administration)	department store
*八佰伴	Baat˗(eight)	baakˉ(hundred)	boon˗(friend)		Yaohan (a Japanese department store)

*"佰" is a variant form of "百", used exclusively in numbers.

Yale System : baak, Baakgàai, baakfo gùngsī, Baatbaakbuhn

Lau System : baak³, Baak³ gaai¹, baak³ foh³ gung¹ si¹⁰, Baat³ baak³ boon⁶

Pinyin : bǎi, Bǎijiā, bǎihuò gōngsī, Bābǎibàn

| | Sai` | | West | |

西

| 一 | 厂 | 厅 | 丙 | 西 | 西 |

西港城
WESTERN MARKET
SHOPPING MALL BUSINESS HOURS
FROM 10.00 AM - 7.00 PM (MON-SUN)

西人	sai` (west)	yan` (man)		westerner
西環	Sai` (west)	Waan` (circuit)		Western District
西貢	Sai` (west)	gung— (tribute)		Sai Kung (district in New Territories)
西港城	Sai` (west)	gong´ (harbour)	sing` (city)	Western Market

Yale System : sài, sàiyàhn, SàiWàahn, Sàigung, Sàigóng Sìhng

Lau System : sai¹, sai¹ yan⁴, Sai¹ waan⁴ Sai¹ gung³, Sai¹ gong² Sing⁴

Pinyin : xī, xīrén, Xīhuán, Xīgòng, Xī gǎng Chéng

59

地　　Dei‿　　ground

一　十　土　圠　圸　地

地庫	dei‿ (ground)	foo— (warehouse)		basement
地產	dei‿ (ground)	chaan╱ (property)		real estate property (on real estate agent signs)
跑馬地	Paaw╱ (running)	maa╱ (horse)	dei‿ (dei╱) (place)	Happy Valley
置地廣場	jee— (set up)	dei‿ (land)	gwong╱ cheung╲ (vast ground)	the Landmark

---

Yale System : deih, deihfu, deihcháan, Páaumáhdeih, Jideih Gwóngchèuhng

Lau System : dei[6], dei[6] fu[3], dei[6] chaan[2], Paau[2] ma[5] dei[6], Ji[3] dei[6] Gwong[2] cheuhng[4]

Pinyin : dì, dìkù, dìchǎn, Páomǎdì, Zhìdì Guǎngchǎng

行	Hang、	walk
	Hong /	firm
	Hong、	

ノ	⺁	彳	彳	行	行

行人路	hang、(walk)	yan、(man)	lou_ (path)	pavement
金行	gam¯ (gold)	hong / (firm)		jewellery shop
車行	che、(car)	hong / (firm)		car company
銀行	ngan、(silver)	hong、(firm)		bank

Yale System : hàhng, hàhngyàhn louh, gāmhóng, chèhóng, ngàhn hòhng
Lau System : hang⁴, hang⁴ yan⁴ lo⁶, gam¹⁰ hong², che¹ hong², ngan⁴ hong⁴
Pinyin : xíng, xíngrén lù, jīnháng, chē háng, yín háng

年　　Neenˋ　year

| ノ | ⺊ | ⺈ | ⺈ | 幺 | 年 |

週年	jauˋ (cycle)	neenˋ (year)		anniversary
青年會	Chingˋ (young)	neenˋ year	Wooy´ (association)	YMCA
明年	mingˋ (bright)	neenˋ (year)		next year
新年	sanˋ (new)	neenˋ (year)		New Year

Yale System : nìhn, jàunìhn, Chìngnìhn Wúi, mìhngnìhn, sànnìhn
Lau System : nin⁴, jau¹ nin⁴, Ching¹ nin⁴ wooi², ming⁴ nin⁴, san¹ nin⁴
Pinyin : nían, zhōunián, Qīngnián Huì, míngnián, xīnnián

沙 Saaˋ sand

尖沙咀
Tsim Sha Tsui

| ˋ | ⼫ | 氵 | 沙 | 沙 | 沙 | 沙 |

沙田　　Saaˋ　　teenˋ　　　　　　Shatin
　　　　(sand　 rice field)

尖沙咀　Jeemˋ　saaˋ　jeuy´　　　Tsimshatsui
　　　　(pointed sand　mouth)

沙灘　　Saaˋ　　taanˋ　　　　　　beach (on signs)
　　　　(sand　 water area)

沙頭角　Saaˋ　　Tauˋ　　Gok−　　Sha Tau Kok (district in New Territories)
　　　　(sand　 head　 corner)

Yale System　:　sà, Sàtìhn, Jìmsàjéui, sà tàan, Sà Tàuh Gok
Lau System　 :　sa¹, Sa¹ tin⁴, Jim¹ sa¹ jui², sa¹ taan¹, Sa¹ Tau⁴ Gok³
Pinyin　　　 :　shā, Shātián, Jiānshāzuǐ, shātān, Shā Tóu Jiǎo

車　Chè　vehicle

车

一 ⌐ 斤 斤 百 亘 車

泊車	paak⁻ (park	chè car)	park the car (on signboards)
電車	deen⁻ (electric	chè car)	tram
私家車	see` (private	gaa⁻ family	chè car)	private car
停車場	ting` (stop	chè car	cheung spacious area)	carpark

Yale System : chè, paak chè, dihnchè, sìgā chè, tìhngchèchèuhng

Lau System : che¹, paak³ che¹, din⁶ che¹, si¹ ga¹⁰ che¹, ting⁴ che¹ cheung⁴

Pinyin : chē, bó chē, diàn chē, sījiā chē, tíngchēchǎng

折　　Jeet –　　discount (on sales notices)

一　丁　才　扩　扩　折　折

七折	chat – (seven)	jeet – discount)	30% discount (Lit. 7/10)
八折	baat – (eight)	jeet – discount)	20% discount (Lit. 8/10)
九折	gau ╱ (nine)	jeet – discount)	10% discount (Lit. 9/10)
八五折	baat – (eight)	ng ╱ five	jeet – discount)	15% discount (Lit 8.5/10)

Yale System　:　jit, chātjit, baatjit, gáujit, baatńghjit
Lau System　:　jit³, chat¹⁰ jit, baat³ jit³, gau² jit³, baat³ ng⁵ jit³
Pinyin　:　zhé, qīzhé, bāzhé, jiǔzhé, bāwǔzhé

邨　　Chün⁻　estate

一　丆　丏　丯　邔　邨　邨

杏花邨	Hang₋ (apricot)	faa` flower	Chün⁻ estate)	Heng Fa Chuen (district on HK Island Line)
華富邨	Waa` (Chinese)	foo⁻ wealth	Chün⁻ estate)	Wa Fu Estate (district on HK side)
彩虹邨	Choi´ (colourful)	hung` rainbow	Chün⁻ estate)	Choi Hung Estate (district on Kln. side)
綠楊新邨	Luk₋ (gree	yeung`	San` new	Chün⁻ estate)	Luk Yeung Sun Chuen (district on Tsuen Wan side)

Yale System : chyūn, Hahng fà Chyūn, Wàh fu Chyūn, Chói hùhng Chyūn, Luhk yèuhng Sàn Chyūn

Lau System : chuen[10], Hang[6] fa[1] Chuen[10], Wa[4] fu[3] Chuen[10], Choi[2] hung[4] Chuen[10], Luk[6] yeung[4] San[1] chuen[10]

Pinyin : cūn, Xìng huā Cūn, Huá fù Cūn, Cǎi hóng Cūn, Lǜ yáng Xīn Cūn

村

局 Guk‿, council, establishment
(or Guk´ for all items below)

POST OFFICE
郵 政 局

| 丁 | 刁 | 尸 | 尸 | 局 | 局 | 局 |

書局　sü╲　　guk‿　　　　　　　bookstore
　　　(book　establishment)

消防局　Syu╲　fong╲　Guk‿　　Fire Services Department
　　　(extinguish prevent council)

郵政局　Yau╲　jing—　Guk‿　　Post Office
　　　(post administration council)

招商局　Jyu╲　seung╲　Guk‿　China Merchants Steam Navigation Company
　　　(Invite merchant Bereau)

Yale System : guhk, syùguhk, Sìufòhng Guhk, Yàuhjing Guhk, Jìu Sèung Guhk
Lau System : guk⁶, sue¹ guk⁶, Siu¹ fong⁴ Guk⁶, Yau⁴ jing³ Guk⁶, Jiu¹ Seung¹ Guk⁶
Pinyin : jú, shūjú, Xiāofáng Jú, Yóuzhèng Jú, Zhāo shāng Jú

門　　Moon` door
门

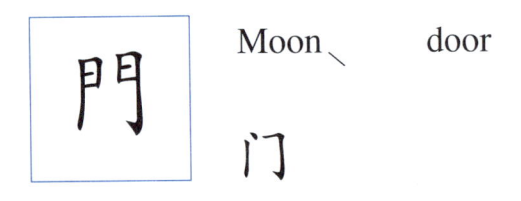

| 丨 | 冂 | 冂 | 冃 | 冃ᴸ | 冃ᴸ | 門 |

中門　　jung` moon`　　　　middle door (notice in bus)
　　　　(middle) (door)

澳門　　Ou− moon`　　　　Macau
　　　　(Quarry) (door)

車門　　che` moon`　　　　vehicle door (bus, MTR, tram, etc)
　　　　(vehicle) (door)

太平門　taay− ping` moon`　emergency exit
　　　　(peace) (door)

Yale System : mùhn, jùng mùhn, Oumùhn, chèmùhn, taaipìhng mùhn

Lau System : moon⁴, jung¹ moon⁴, O³ moon⁴, che¹ moon⁴, taai³ ping⁴ moon⁴

Pinyin　　 : mén, zhōng mén, Aòmén, chēmén, tàipíng mén

角　　　Gok−　　　point of land

丿　ク　ゲ　서　角　角　角

北角	Bak⁻ (north)	gok⁻ point of land)		North Point (HK Island)
旺角	Wong_ (prosperous)	gok⁻ point of land)		Mongkok (Kowloon)
牛頭角	Ngau╲ (ox)	tau╲ head)	gok⁻ point of land)	Ngau Tau Kok (Kowloon)
荔枝角	Lai_ (	jee⁻ laichee	gok⁻ point of land)	Lai Chi Kok (Kowloon)

Yale System　:　gok, Bākgok, Wohngok, Ngàuhtàuhgok, Laihjīgok
Lau System　:　gok³, Bak¹⁰ gok³, Wong⁶ gok³, Ngau⁴ tau⁴ gok³, Lai⁶ ji¹⁰ gok³
Pinyin　　　:　jiǎo, Běijiǎo, Wàngjiǎo, Niútóujiǎo, Lìzhījiǎo

防　　Fong丶　prevent

消防車出路
FIRE APPLIANCE EXIT

㇀　㇁　阝　阝丶　阝⁻　防　防

| 消防局 | syu丶 (diminish) | fong丶 (prevent) | guk⁻ (bereau) | | fireman |

| 防火設備 | fong丶 (prevent) | for´ fire | chit⁻ set | bei⁻ prepare) | fire prevention facility |

| 防風措施 | fong丶 (prevent) | fung` wind | chou⁻ | see丶 measure) | typhoon prevention measure |

Yale System : fòhng, sìufòhng guhk, fòhng fó chitbeih, fòhngfùng chousì

Lau System : fong⁴, siu¹ fong⁴ guk⁶, fong⁴ foh² chit³ bei⁶, fong⁴ fung¹ cho³ si¹

Pinyin　　　: fáng, xiāofáng jú, fánghuó shèbèi, fángfēng cuòshī

| | Deem– | | shop | |

店

| 丶 | 亠 | 广 | 广 | 庐 | 庐 | 店 | 店 |

快餐店	faay⁻ (fast)	chaan⁻ meal	deem⁻ shop)	fast food shop
找換店	jaaw╱ (change)	woon⁻ swap	deem⁻ shop)	money changer
免稅店	Meen╱ (exempted)	seuy⁻ tax	deem⁻ shop)	Duty-free shop
便利店	been⁻ (convenient)	lei⁻	deem⁻ store)	convenience store

Yale System : dim, faaichāan dim, jaáuwuhn dim, Míhnseui Dim, bihnleih dim
Lau System : dim³, faai³ chaan¹⁰ dim³, jaau² woon⁶ dim³, Min⁵ sui³ Dim³, Bim⁶ lei⁶ dim³
Pinyin : diàn, Kuàicān diàn, zhǎohuàn diàn, Miǎnshuì Diàn, biànlì diàn

71

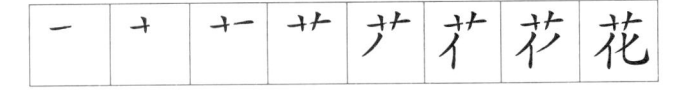

花	Faa˴	flower
	花	

| 一 | 十 | 十 | 艹 | 艹 | 艹 | 花 | 花 |

花店	faa˴ (flower)	deem− shop)		flower shop
花籃	faa˴ (flower)	laam˴ basket)		flower basket
鮮花	seen˴ (fresh)	faa˴ flower)		fresh flowers
花園道	Faa˴ (flower)	yün˴ court	Dou− road)	Garden Road (in Central)

Yale System : fà, fàdim, fà làahm, sìn fà, Fàyùhn Douh

Lau System : fa¹, fa¹ dim³, fa¹ laam⁴, sin¹ fa¹, Fa¹ yuen⁴ Do⁶

Pinyin : huā, huādiàn, huālán, xiānfā, Huāyuán Dào

亞	Aa-	the sound 'aa' in foreign words
亚		

| 一 | 丆 | 丅 | 亐 | 疋 | 亚 | 亜 | 亞 |

CENTRE OF ASIAN STUDIES
TANG CHI NGONG BUILDING
亞洲研究中心
鄧志昂樓

亞皆老街	Aa-	gaai`	lou´	Gaai¯ (Street)	Argyle Street
亞厘畢道	Aa-	lei`	bat¯	Dou_ (Road)	Albert Road
東亞銀行	Dung` (East)	aa- Asia	Ngan`	hong` bank)	Bank of East Asia
亞士厘道	Aa-	see¯	lei`	Dou_ (Road)	Ashley Road

Yale System : a, Agàailóuh Gāai, AlèihbahtDouh, Dùng Aa Ngàhnhòhng, Asihleìh Douh

Lau System : a³, A³ gaai¹ lou⁵ Gaai¹, A³ lei⁴ bat⁶ Dou⁶, Dung¹ a³ Ngan⁴ hong⁴, A³ si⁶ lei⁴ dou⁶

Pinyin : yà, Yàjīalǎo Jīe, Yàlíbì Dào, Dōngyà Yínháng, Yàshìlí Dào

73

	Geuy—	object, item
具		(on department store signs)

華光文具印製公司
WAH KWONG STATIONERY PRINTING CO.

| 丨 | 冂 | 冃 | 月 | 目 | 且 | 具 | 具 |

文具	man (language)	geuy— (item)	stationery
皮具	pei (leather)	geuy— (item)	leather ware
玩具	woon— (play)	geuy— (item)	toy
廚具	chü (kitchen)	geuy— (item)	kitchen ware

Yale System   :   geuih, màhngeuih, pèihgeuih, wuhngeuih, chyùhgeuih

Lau System   :   gui⁶, man⁴ gui⁶, pei⁴ gui⁶, woon⁶ gui⁶, chue⁴ gui⁶

Pinyin   :   jù, wénjù, píjù, wánjù, chújù

| 往 | Wong / to (toward) (on direction signs) |

往荃灣 →
Trains towards Tsuen Wan

| ✓ | ⁊ | 彳 | 彳 | 行 | 行 | 往 | 往 |

往九龍	wong / (to	Gau / nine	lung \ dragon)		to Kowloon
往中環	wong / (to	Jung \ central	waan \ enclosure)		to Central District
往香港	wong / (to	Heung \ fragrant	gong / harbour)		to Hong Kong
往停車場	wong / (to	ting \ stopping	che \ car	cheung \ spacious area)	to carpark

Yale System : wóhng, wóhng Gáulùhng, wóhng Jùngwàahn, wóhng Hèunggóng, wóhng tìhngchèchèuhng

Lau System : wong⁵, wong⁵ Gau² lung⁴, wong⁵ Jung¹ waan⁴, wong⁵ Heung¹ gong², wong⁵ ting⁴che¹ cheung⁴

Pinyin : wǎng, wǎng Jiǔlóng, wǎng Zhōnghuán, wǎng Xiānggǎng, wǎng tíngchēchǎng

75

| 金 | Gam⁻ gold |

| ノ | 八 | 人 | 仐 | 仐 | 余 | 余 | 金 |

黃金	wong ╲ (yellow)	gam⁻ (gold)	gold
金行	gam⁻ (gold)	hong ╱ (firm)	goldsmith's shop
金鐘	Gam⁻ (gold)	jung⁻ (bell)	Admiralty
美金	mei ╱ (America)	gam⁻ (gold)	American dollar

Yale System : gām, wòhnggām, gām hóng, Gāmjūng, méihgām
Lau System : gam[10], wong[4] gam[10], gam[10] hong[2], Gam[10] jung[10], mei[5] gam[10]
Pinyin : jīn, huángjīn, jīn háng, Jīnzhōng, Měijīn

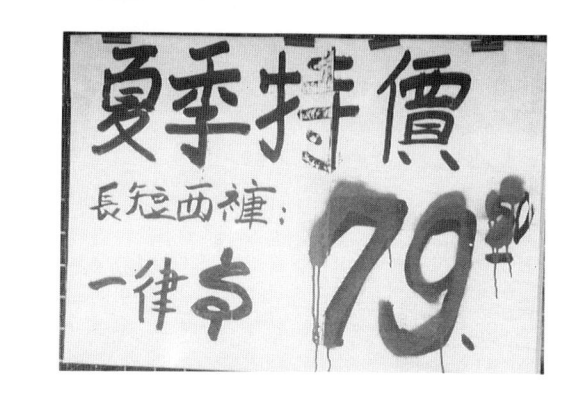

季   Gwai-   season

| 一 | 二 | 千 | 禾 | 禾 | 季 | 季 | 季 |

春季	cheunˋ (spring)	gwai- season)	spring
夏季	haa— (summer)	gwai- season)	summer
秋季	chauˋ (autumn)	gwai- season)	autumn
冬季	dungˋ (winter)	gwai- season)	winter

Yale System : gwai, chèungwai, hahgwai, chàugwai, dùnggwai

Lau System : gwai³, chun¹ gwai³, ha⁶ gwai³, chau¹ gwai³, dung¹ gwai³

Pinyin : jì, chūnjì, xiàjì, qiūjì, dōngjì

77

| 東 | Dungˋ | east |

东

| 一 | 丆 | 丐 | 盲 | 苜 | 車 | 東 | 東 |

東方紅	Dungˋ (east)	fongˋ direction	hungˊ red)		Dung Fong Hung Chinese Medicine
東區走廊	Dungˋ (east)	keuyˊ district	jauˊ run	longˊ corridor)	East Corridor
東邊街	Dungˋ (east)	beenˊ side	Gaaiˉ street)		Eastern Street
東區隧道	Dungˋ (east)	keuyˊ district	seuy_ hollow	dou_ road)	East Harbour Tunnel

Yale System : dùng, Dùng fòng Hùhng, Dùng kèui Jáulòhng, Dùngbīn Gāai, Dùng Kèui Seuihdouh

Lau System : dung¹, Dung¹ fong¹ hung⁴, Dung¹ kui¹ Jau² long⁴, Dung¹ bin¹ Gaai¹⁰, Dung¹ kui¹ Sui⁶ do⁶

Pinyin : dōng, Dōngfāng Hóng, Dōng Qū Zǒuláng, Dōngbiān Jiē, Dōng Qū Suìdào

音　　Yamˋ　　audio; sound

志力影音　ONE HOUR PHOTO FINISHING.
CHEERPOWER CAMERA & AUDIO

| 丶 | 亠 | 立 | 立 | 立 | 产 | 音 | 音 | 音 |

音樂會　Yamˋ　ngok_　wooy´　concert
　　　　(　　music　　gathering)
音響　　yamˋ　heung´　Hi-fi (shop signs for Hi-fi shops)
　　　　(audio　sound-making)
收音機　Sauˋ　yamˋ　geiˋ　radio
　　　　(receive　sound　machine)
影音　　ying´　yamˋ　video & Hi-fi (shops signs for video & Hi-fi shops)
　　　　(visual　audio)

Yale System : yàm, yàmngohkwúi, yàmhéung, sàuyàmgèi yíngyàm
Lau System : yam¹, yam¹ ngok⁶ wooi², yam¹ heung², sau¹ yam¹ gei¹, ying² yam¹
Pinyin : yīn, yīnyuèhuì, yīnxiǎng, shōuyīnjī, yǐngyīn

79

美　　　Mei╱　　beautiful

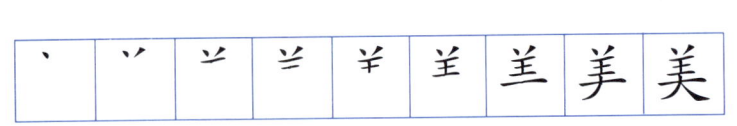

| 丶 | 丷 | 兰 | 亼 | 羊 | 芏 | 兰 | 羊 | 美 |

美心　　Mei╱　　sam╲
　　　　(beautiful)　(heart)　　　　Maxim's (a bakery/restaurant chain)

美孚　　Mei╱　　foo╲
　　　　　　　　　　　　　　　　　Mei Foo (An MTR stop on Tsuen Wan Line)

美國　　Mei╱　　gwok—
　　　　(beautiful)　(country)　　U.S.A.

美麗華　Mei╱　　lai—　　waa╲
　　　　　　　　　　　　　　　　　Miramar (Hotel)

Yale System : méih, Méihsàm, Méihfù, Méihgwok, Méihlaihwàh

Lau System : mei[5], Mei[5] sam[1], Mei[5] foo[1], Mei[5] gwok[3], Meih[5] lai[6] wa[4]

Pinyin : měi, Měixīn, Měifú, Měiguó, Měilìhuá

| 洲 | Jau ˋ | continent |

往長洲
CHEUNG CHAU

| ˋ | ˙˙ | 氵 | 氵 | 沙 | 沙 | 洲 | 洲 | 洲 |

亞洲	Aa—	jau ˋ (continent)	Asia
美洲	Mei ╱	jau ˋ (continent)	America
歐洲	Au ˋ	jau ˋ (continent)	Europe
澳洲	Ou—	Jau ˋ (continent)	Australia

Yale System : jàu, A jàu, Méihjàu, Àujàu, Oujàu
Lau System : jau¹, A³ jau¹, Mei⁵ jau¹, Au¹ jau¹, Ou³ jau¹
Pinyin : zhōu, Yàzhōu, Měizhōu, Ōuzhōu, Àozhōu

洗　　Sai ́　　wash

| 丶 | 冫 | 氵 | 氵 | 汇 | 汄 | 洰 | 浂 | 洗 |

洗手間	sai ́ (wash)	sau ́ hand	gaan ‾ area	washroom (on washroom doors)
洗衣機	sai ́ (wash)	yee ˋ clothing	gei ˋ machine	washing machine
洗衣店	sai ́ (wash)	yee ˋ clothing	deem ‾ shop	laundry shop
乾洗	gon ˋ (dry)	sai ́ wash)		dry cleaning (on laundry shop signs)

Yale System : sái, sáisáugāan, sáiyìgèi, gònsái
Lau System : sai², sai² sau² gaan¹⁰, sai² yi¹ gei¹, sai² yi¹ dim³, gon¹ sai²
Pinyin : xǐ, xǐshǒujiān, xǐyījī, xǐyīdiàn, gānxǐ

室　　Sat⁻　　room

| 丶 | 丷 | 宀 | 宀 | 宊 | 宎 | 宨 | 室 | 室 |

咖啡室	gaa⁻	fe⁻	sat⁻ (room)		coffee shop
試身室	see⁻ (try)	sanˋ body	sat⁻ room)		fitting room
辦公室	baanˍ (handle)	gungˋ public	sat⁻ room)		office
室內設計	sat⁻ (room)	noiˍ inside	cheet⁻ establish	gai⁻ calculate)	interior design

Yale System : sāt, gafēsāt, sisàn sāt, baahngùngsāt, sātnoih chitgai
Lau System : sat¹⁰, ga³ fe¹⁰ sat¹⁰, si³ san¹ sat¹⁰, baan⁶ gung¹ sat¹⁰, sat¹⁰ noi⁶ chit³ gai³
Pinyin : shì, kāfēi shì, shìshēn shì, bàngōngshì, shì'nèi shèjì

城	Singˋ　city

海港城

| 一 | 十 | 土 | 土ˊ | 圵 | 圴 | 城 | 城 | 城 |

城巴	Singˋ (city)	Baaˉ bus)		City Bus
潮州城	Chyuˋ (Chaozhou)	jauˋ	singˋ castle)	Chiuchow City (name of restaurant)
九龍城	Gauˊ (nine	lungˋ dragon	Singˋ city)	Kowloon City
海港城	Hoiˊ (ocean	gongˊ harbour	Singˋ city)	Harbour City

Yale System : sìhng, Sìhng Bā, Chìujàu Sìhng, Gáulùhng Sìhng, Hóigóng Sìhng

Lau System : sing⁴, Sing⁴ Ba¹⁰, Chiu⁴ jau¹ Sing⁴, Gau² lung⁴ Sing⁴, Hoi² gong² Sing⁴

Pinyin : chéng, Chéng Bā, Cháozhōu Chéng, Jiǔlóng Chéng, Hǎigǎng Chéng

星 Sing` star

星光行

| 丶 | 冂 | 冃 | 日 | 旦 | 旦 | 早 | 旱 | 星 |

星洲 (新加坡)　Sing` jau` (San` gaa⁻ bor⁻)　Singapore

星光行　　　　Sing` gwong` Hong´　　Star House (near Star Ferry Kowloon)
　　　　　　　(star) (bright) (firm)

星期日　　　　Sing` kei´ yat_　　　　Sunday
　　　　　　　(star) (period) (day)

天星小輪　　　Teen` Sing` Syu´ leun´　Star Ferry
　　　　　　　(sky) (star) (small) (ferry)

Yale System　:　sìng, sìngjàu, Sìnggwòng Hóng, Sìngkèihyaht, Tìnsìng Síulèuhn

Lau System　:　sing¹, Sing¹ jau¹, Sing¹ gwong¹ Hong², Sing¹ Kei⁴ yat⁶, Ting¹ sing¹ Siu² lun⁴

Pinyin　　　:　xīng, Xīngzhōu, Xīngguāng Háng, Xīngqīrì, Tiānxīng Xiǎolún

品 Ban′ article, thing

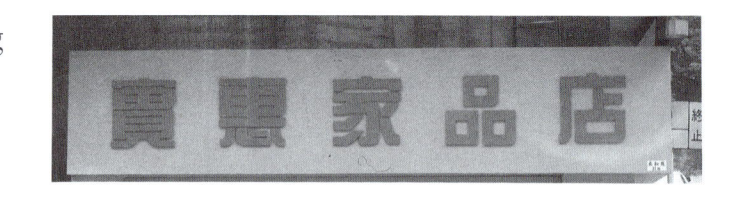

用品	yung‿ (use)	ban′ (article)	household (shop sign)
食品	sik‿ (eat)	ban′ (article)	food (shop sign)
飲品	yam′ (drink)	ban′ (article)	drinks (on menu)
工藝品	gung` (manual)	ngai‿ (art) ban′ (article)	handicraft

Yale System : bán, yuhngbán, sihkbán, yámbán, gùngngaihbán
Lau System : ban², yung⁶ ban², sik⁶ ban², yam² ban², gung¹ ngai⁶ ban²
Pinyin : pǐn, yòngpǐn, shípǐn, yǐnpǐn, gōngyìpǐn

香　　Heung` fragrant

春季香水

| 一 | 二 | 千 | 千 | 禾 | 禾 | 杳 | 香 | 香 |

香港　　Heung` gong´　　　　　　Hong Kong
　　　(fragrant) (harbour)

香港仔　Heung` gong´ jai´　　　Aberdeen (on Hong Kong Island)
　　　(fragrant) (harbour) (small)

香水　　heung` seuy´　　　　　　perfume (on notices)
　　　(fragrant) (water)

香煙　　heung` yeen⁻　　　　　　cigarette (on advertisements)
　　　(fragrant) (smoke)

Yale System : hèung, Hèung góng, Hèung góng jái, hèung séui, hèung yīn
Lau System : heung[1], Heung[1] gong[2], Heung[1] gong[2] jai[2], heung[1] sui[2], heung[1] yin[10]
Pinyin : xiāng, Xiāng gǎng, Xiāng gǎng zǎi, xiāng shuǐ, xiāng yān

87

界 Gaay– side; boundary

| 丶 | 冂 | 冋 | 用 | 田 | 毘 | 界 | 界 | 界 |

新界	Sàn (new)	gaay– (boundary)	New Territory
男界	naam (male)	gaay– (side)	gentlemen's restroom
女界	neuy (female)	gaay– (side)	lady's restroom
界限街	Gaay– (boundary)	haan (limit)	Gaay (street)	Boundary Street

Yale System: gaai, Sàn gaai, nàahm gaai, néuih gaai, Gaai haahn Gāai

Lau System: gaai³, San¹ gaai³, naam⁴ gaai³, nui⁵ gaai³, Gaai³ haan⁶ Gaai¹⁰

Pinyin: jiè, Xīnjiè, nán jiè, nǔjiè, Jièxiàn Jiē

88

家　　Gaa⁻　　family

`、` `丷` `宀` `宀` `宀` `宀` `宀` `家` `家` `家`

Private Road 私家路

酒家	jau ╱ (wine)	gaa ⁻ (family)		Chinese restaurant
大家樂	Daay _ (big)	gaa ⁻ (family)	lok _ (happy)	Cafe de Coral (a fast food chain)
私家車	see ╲ (private)	gaa ⁻ (family)	che ╲ (car)	private car (road signs)
家庭用品	gaa ╲ (family)	ting ╲	yung _ (use)	ban ╱ (item)	household goods

Yale System : gā, jáugā, Daaihgālohk, sìgāchè, gàtìhng yuhngbán
Lau System : ga¹⁰, jau² ga¹⁰, Daai⁶ ga¹⁰ lok⁶, si¹ ga¹⁰ che¹, ga¹ ting⁴ yung⁶ ban²
Pinyin : jiā, jiǔjiā, Dàjiālè, sījiā chē, jiātíng yòngpǐn

| 酒 | Jau´ | wine |

Hotel Entrance 酒店入口

| 丶 | 丷 | 氵 | 汀 | 汀 | 沂 | 沔 | 洒 | 洒 | 酒 |

酒店	jau´ (wine)	deem⁻ (shop)	hotel
酒家	jau´ (wine)	gaa⁻ (family)	Chinese restaurant
酒吧	jau´ (alcoholics)	baa⁻ (bar)	bar
啤酒	be⁻	jau´ (wine)	beer (on menu)

Yale System : jáu, jáudim, jáugā, jáubā, bējáu

Lau System : jau², jau² dim³, jau² ga¹⁰, jau² ba¹⁰, be¹⁰ jau²

Pinyin : jiǔ, jiǔdiàn, jiǔjiā, jiǔbā, píjiǔ

海 Hói sea

OCEAN CENTRE 海洋中心

丶 丶 氵 氻 沪 汇 浹 海 海 海

海洋公園　Hói yeuhng Gùng yún　Ocean Park (an amusement park on Hong Kong Island)
　　　　　(sea ocean　park)

海鮮　　　hói seen　　fresh sea-food (restaurant sign)
　　　　　(sea fresh)

上海　　　Seuhng hói　Shanghai
　　　　　(on sea)

海底隧道　Hói dai seuy dou　Cross Harbour Tunnel
　　　　　(sea bottom tunnel road)

Yale System : hói, Hóiyeùhng Gùngyún, hóisìn, seuhnghói, Hóihái Seuihdouh
Lau System : hoi[2], Hoi[2] yeung[4] Gung[1] yuen[2], hoi[2] sin[1], Seung[6] hoi[2], Hoi[2] dai[2] sui[6] do[6]
Pinyin : hǎi, Hǎiyáng Gōngyuán, hǎixiān, Shànghǎi, Hǎidǐ Sùidào

| 座 | Jor_ | housing block; seat (in theatre) |

| 、 | 亠 | 广 | 广 | 庀 | 庀 | 庐 | 座 | 座 | 座 |

A 座	Ei ¯ (A	Jor_ block)		Block A
第一座	Dai _ (order	yat ¯ one	Jor_ block)	Block I
第二座	Dai _ (order	yee _ two	Jor_ block)	Block II
第三座	Dai _ (order	saam ＼ three	Jor_ block)	Block III
滿座	moon ╱ (full	jor _ seat)		full house

Yale System : joh, Ēi Joh, Daihyāt Joh, Daihyih Joh, Daihsàam Joh, múhn joh

Lau System : joh[6], Ei[10] Joh[6], Dai[6] yat[10] Joh[6], Dai[6] yi[6] Joh[6], Dai[6] saam[1] Joh[6], moon[5] joh[6]

Pinyin : zuò, Ēi Zuò, Dìyī Zuò, Dì'èr Zuò, Dìsān Zuò, mǎn zuò

| 高 | | Gòu | high |

| 丶 | 亠 | 宀 | 亯 | 肓 | 戸 | 高 | 高 | 高 | 高 |

高級	goù (high)	kap⁻ (grade)			high quality
最高法院	Jeuy⁻ (most)	goù (high)	Faat_ (law)	yün´ (court)	Supreme Court
高層地庫	goù (high)	chang⁻ (storey)	dei_ (ground)	foo⁻ (vault)	upper basement
的士高	dik⁻	see_	goù		disco

Yale System : gòu, gòu kāp, Jeuigòu Faatyún, gòuchàhng deihfu, dīksihgòu

Lau System : go¹, go¹ kap¹⁰, Jui³ go¹, Faat³ yuen², go¹ chang⁴ dei⁶ foo³, dik¹⁰ si⁶ go¹

Pinyin : gāo, gāo jí, Juìgāo Fǎyuàn, gāocéng dìkù, dìshìgāo

站 Jaam˩ station, stop

Central Station 中環站

| 丶 | 亠 | 亠 | 立 | 立 | 立 | 立 | 站 | 站 |

巴士站	baa˧	see˥	jaam˩ (stop)	bus stop
的士站	dik˧	see˥	jaam˩ (stop)	taxi stand
電車站	deen˩ (electricity)	che˥ car	jaam˩ stop)	tram stop
纜車站	laam˩ (cable	che˥ car	jaam˩ station)	peak tram station

Yale System : jaahm, bāsí jaahm, dīksí jaahm, dihnchè jaahm, laahmchè jaahm

Lau System : jaam⁶, ba¹⁰ si² jaahm⁶, dik¹⁰ si² jaam⁶, din⁶ che¹ jaam⁶ laam⁶ che¹ jaam⁶

Pinyin : zhàn, bāshì zhàn, dìshìzhàn, diànzhēzhàn, lǎnchēzhàn

茶　　Chaaˋ　tea

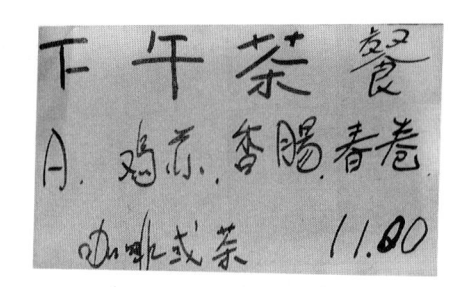

茶

| 一 | 十 | 十 | 艹 | 艹 | 艾 | 苂 | 苓 | 茶 | 茶 |

茶樓	chaaˋ (tea	lauˋ building)		teahouse
奶茶	naay´ (milk	chaaˋ tea)		tea with milk (on menu)
飲茶	yam´ (drink	chaaˋ tea)		to have Chinese tea and dim-sum
涼茶	leungˋ (cool	chaaˋ tea)		herb tea

Yale System : chàh, chàlàuh, náaih chàh, yám chàh, lèuhngchàh

Lau System : cha[4], cha[4] lau[4], naai[5] cha[4], yam[2] cha[4], leung[4] cha[4]

Pinyin : chá, chálóu, nǎi chá, yǐn chá, liángchá

時　seeˋ　　　hour
时

｜ 冂 月 日 日⁻ 日⁺ 旪 旪 時 時

一小時	yat⁻ (one)	syu´ small	seeˋ hour)	one hour (film)
上午十時	seung_ (upper)	ng´ noon	sap_ ten	seeˋ hour)	10a.m. (spoken: sap_ deem´)
下午五時	haa_ (lower)	ng´ noon	ng´ five	seeˋ hour)	5p.m. (spoken: ng´ deem´)
晚上九時	maan´ (evening)	seung_ on	gau´ nine	seeˋ hour)	9p.m. (spoken: gau´ deem´)
時間廊	seeˋ (time)	gaan⁻	longˋ corridor)	City Chain (a watch chain store)

Yale System : sìh, yāt síusìh, seuhngńgh sahpsìh, hahngh ńghsìh, máahnseuhng gáusìh, sìhgaanlòhng

Lau System : si⁴, yat¹⁰ siu² si⁴, seung⁶ ng⁵ sap⁶ si⁴, ha⁶ ng⁵ ng⁵ si⁴, maan⁵ seung⁶ gau², si⁴ si⁴ gaan³ long⁴

Pinyin : shí, yì xiǎoshí, shàngwǔ shíshí, xiàwǔ wǔshí, wǎnshàng jiǔshí, shíjiān Láng

96

Dou ´   island

島

島

| ´ | 丨 | 冂 | 户 | 户 | 自 | 鸟 | 鸟 | 岛 | 岛 |

往南丫島
TO LAMMA ISLAND

半島	boon— (half)	dou´ (island)		peninsula (also name of a hotel)
港島	Gong´ (Hong Kong)	Dou´ (island)		Hong Kong Island
南丫島	Naam` (south)	aa` (fork)	Dou´ (island)	Lamma Island
青衣島	Ching` (green)	Yee` (clothes)	Dou´ (island)	Tsing Yi Island

Yale System : dóu, bundóu, Góng Dóu, Nàahm-À, Dóu, Chìng Yì Dóu

Lau System   : do², boon³ do², Gong² Do², Naam⁴ A¹ Do², Ching¹ Yi¹ Do²

Pinyin   : dǎo, bàndǎo, Gǎng Dǎo, Nán Yā Dǎo, Qīng Yī Dǎo

租	Jou` rent
	(on estate agents' signs)

| ㇒ | 二 | 千 | 禾 | 禾 | 利 | 和 | 租 | 租 | 租 |

租售	jou` (rent)	sau¯ (sell)	to let or to sell
出租	cheut¯ (out)	jou` (rent)	to let
平租	peng` (cheap)	jou` (rent)	cheap rental
招租	jiu` (invite)	jou` (rent)	to let

Yale System : jòu, jòusauh, chēutjòu, pèhngjòu, jiujòu

Lau System : jo¹, jo¹ sau⁶, chut¹⁰ jou¹, peng⁴ jou¹, jiu¹ jou¹

Pinyin : zū, zūshòu, chūzū, píngzū, zhāozū

院　　Yün´　　a courtyard

丶　㇇　阝　阝　阝　阡　阡　阬　陊　院

書院	sü` (book)	yün´ (courtyard)			college
戲院	hei— (show)	yün´ (courtyard)			cinema
港安醫院	Góng´ (Hong)	On— (Kong)	Yee` (Safety)	yün´ (hospital)	Hong Kong Adventist Hospital
法院	faat— (law)	yün´ (Courtyard)			law court

Yale System : yún, syùyún, heiyún, Góng Ōn Yìyún, faatyún

Lau System : yuen², sue¹ yuen², hei³ yuen², Gong² On¹⁰ Yi¹ yuen², faat³ yuen²

Pinyin : yuàn, shūyuàn, xìyuàn, Gǎng Ān Yīyuàn, fǎyuàn

准　　Jeun´　　permit

丶　亠　丷　扌　才　汁　佇　佐　准　准

不准掉頭　　Bat¯　jeun´　diu_　tau﹨　　　No U-turn
　　　　　　(not)　(permit)　(turn)　(head)

不准停車等候　Bat¯　jeun´　ting﹨　che　dang´　hau_　　No waiting
　　　　　　(not)　(permit)　(stop)　(vehicle)　(wait)　(time)

不准右轉　　Bat¯　jeun´　yau_　jyün–　　No right turn
　　　　　　(not)　(permit)　(right)　(turn)

不准企立　　Bat¯　jeun´　kei´　lap_　　No standing (on bus)
　　　　　　(not)　(permit)　　　(stand)

Yale System: jéun, Bāt jeún diuhtàuh, Bāt jéun tìhng chè dánghauh, Bāt jeún yauh jyun, Bāt jéun kéihlahp

Lau System: jun², Bāt¹⁰ jun² diu⁶ tau⁴, Bāt¹⁰ jun² ting⁴ che¹ dang² hau⁶, Bāt¹⁰ jun² yau⁶ juen³, Bāt¹⁰ jun² kei⁵ lap⁶

Pinyin: zhǔn, Bù zhǔn diàotóu, Bù zhǔn tíng chē děnghòu, Bù zhǔn yòu zhuǎn, Bù zhǔn qǐlì

部

Bou_ department (in department store)

男裝部	naam\ (male	jong¯ style	bou_ department)	men's wear department
女裝部	neuy/ (female	jong¯ style	bou_ department)	ladies' wear department
文具部	man\ (language	geuy_ tool	bou_ department)	stationery department
電器部	deen_ (electricity	hei– utensil	bou_ department)	home electrical appliances department

---

Yale System : bouh, nàahmjōng bouh, néuihjōng bouh, màhngeuih bouh, dihnhei bouh

Lau System : bo^6, $naam^4$ $jong^{10}$ bo^6, nui^5 $jong^{10}$ bo^6, man^4 gui^6 bo^6, din^6 hei^3 bo^6

Pinyin : bù, nánzhuāng bù, nǚzhuāng bù, wénjù bù, diànqì bù

| 厕 | Chee− | toilet, lavatory |

厕

| 一 | 厂 | 厂 | 厈 | 厊 | 厊 | 眉 | 厊 | 厊 | 厕 | 厕 |

厕所	chee− (toilet)	sor´ (place)	toilet
公厕	gung` (public)	chee− (toilet)	public lavatory
女厕	neuy´ (female)	chee− (toilet)	female toilet
男厕	naam` (male)	chee− (toilet)	male toilet

Yale System : chi, chisó, gùng chi, néuih chi, nàahm chi
Lau System : chi^3, chi^3 so^2, gung^1 chi^3, nui^5 chi^3, naam^4 chi^3
Pinyin : cè, cèsuǒ, gōng cè, nü cè, nán cè

厕

票　　Pyu−　　ticket

一 丆 冂 襾 襾 覀 覀 票 票 票 票

郵票	yau\ (post	peeu− ticket)	stamp
門票	moon\ (door	pyu− ticket)	entrance ticket
購票	kau− (buy	pyu− ticket)	buying tickets
儲值票	chü/ (store	jik_ value	pyu− ticket) stored-value ticket (in MTR)

Yale System : piu, yàuhpiu, mùhnpiu, kaupiu, chyúhjihkpiu, sauhpiuchyu

Lau System : piu³, yau⁴ piu³, moon⁴ piu³, kau³ piu³, chue⁵ jik⁶ piu³, sau⁶ piu³ chue³

Pinyin　　 : piào, yóupiào, ménpiào, gòupiào, chǔzhípiào, shòupiàochù

區   Keuyˋ   district

区

Mid-levels 半山區

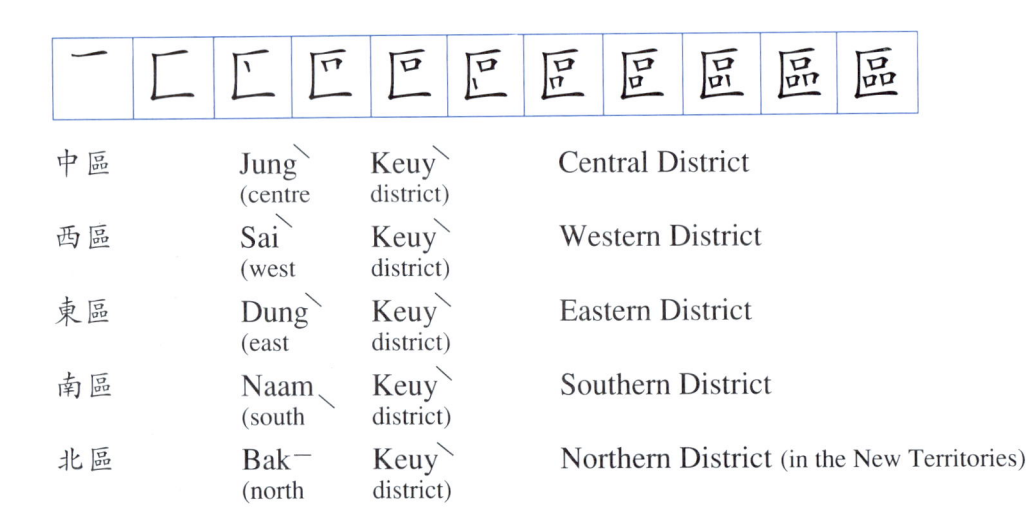

中區	Jungˋ (centre)	Keuyˋ (district)	Central District
西區	Saiˋ (west)	Keuyˋ (district)	Western District
東區	Dungˋ (east)	Keuyˋ (district)	Eastern District
南區	Naamˋ (south)	Keuyˋ (district)	Southern District
北區	Bak¯ (north)	Keuyˋ (district)	Northern District (in the New Territories)

Yale System : Kèui, Jùng Kèui, Sài Kèui, Dùng Kèui, Nàahm Kèui, Bāk Kèui

Lau System : Kui[1], Jung[1] Kui[1], Sai[1] Kui[1], Dung[1] Kui[1], Naam[4] Kui[1], Bak[10] Kui[1]

Pinyin : qū, Zhōng Qū, Xī Qū, Dōng Qū, Nán Qū, Běi Qū

國

Gwok—   country

国

一	冂	冂	冂	同	同	同	或	國	國	國

中國　　Jung ˋ　　　gwok—　　　China
　　　　(centre)　　(country)

美國　　Mei ／　　　gwok—　　　U.S.A.
　　　　(beautiful)　(country)

國貨　　gwok—　　　for—　　　　national products (Chinese Emporium signs)
　　　　(country)　　goods)

國際　　gwok—　　　jai—　　　　international
　　　　(country)　　border)

Yale System : gwok, Jùnggwok, Méihgwok, gwok fo, gwokjai

Lau System : gwok³, Jung¹ gwok³, Mei⁵ gwok³, gwok³ foh³, gwok³ jai³

Pinyin : guó, Zhōngguó, Měiguó, guó huò, guójì

處　Chü–　place
处

| 丶 | 丨 | 卜 | 广 | 户 | 庐 | 虍 | 虎 | 處 | 處 | 處 |

繳費處	gyu╱ (pay)	fai– fee	chü– place)	pay-in counter
補票處	bou╱ (make up)	pyu– ticket	chü– place)	excess fare (office in MTR station)
詢問處	seun╲ (enquire)	man＿ ask	chü– place)	information centre, enquiry
管理處	gwoon╱ (manage)	lei╱ take care	chü– place)	management office (in residential building)

Yale System : chyu, gíufai chyu, bóupiuchyu, sèunmahnchyu, gwúnléihchyu

Lau System : chue³, giu² fai³ chue³, bo² piu³ chue³, sun¹ man⁶ chue³, gwoon² lei⁵ chue³

Pinyin : chù, jiǎofèi chù, bǔpiào chù, xúnwèn chù, guǎnlěi chù

售　　　Sau_　　　　sell (alternative of 賣 Maai_)

旺舖出售
SHOP FOR SALE
店舖代理部
739 1998

| ノ | イ | 亻 | 亻′ | 亻⺊ | 住 | 住 | 佳 | 隹 | 售 | 售 |

售貨員	sau_ (sale)	for— merchandise	yün ˋ person)	shop assistant
出售	cheut¯ (out)	sau_ sell)		for sale (property notice)
平售	peng ˋ (cheap)	sau_ sell)		sale (shop notice)
租售	jou ˋ (rent)	sau_ sell)		to let/for sale

Yale System　：sauh, saufo yùhn, chēutsauh, pèhngsauh, jòusauh
Lau System　：sau⁶, sau⁶ foh³ yuen⁴, chut¹⁰ sau⁶, peng⁴ sau⁶, jou¹ sau⁶
Pinyin　　　：shòu, shòuhuò yuán, chūshòu, píngshòu, zūshòu

107

停　Ting stop
亍

ノ 亻 亻 亻 亻 佇 佇 佇 停 停

停	ting (stop)				stop (traffic sign)
暫停	jaam (temporary)	ting (stop)			temporarily closed (at closed counters)
停車場	ting (stop)	che vehicle	cheung (ground)		car park
緊急停機	gan (tight)	gap urgent	ting stop	gei (machine)	emergency stop (sign beside emergency stop knobs in MTR escalators)

Yale System : tìhng, tìhng, jaahmtìhng, tìhng chè chèuhng, gángāp tìhnggèi

Lau System : ting⁴, ting⁴, jaam⁶ ting⁴, ting⁴ che¹ cheung⁴, gun² gap¹⁰ ting⁴ gei¹

Pinyin : tíng, tíng, zhàntíng, tíngchēchǎng, jǐnjí tíngjī

通									

Tungˋ   pass through

⁻	⁻	⁻	⁻	⁻	⁻	⁻	⁻	⁻	⁻
通									

交通	gaawˋ (cross)	tungˋ (through)	traffic
通道	tungˋ (through)	dou‾ (road)	passage, way
通往	tungˋ (through)	wong╱ (go)	heading for (traffic signs)
通用	tungˋ (through)	yung‾ (use)	common, general

Yale System : tùng, gàautùng, tùngdouh, tùng wóhng, tùngyuhng

Lau System : tung[1], gaau[1] tung[1], tung[1] do[6], tung[1] wong[5], tung[1] yung[6]

Pinyin   : tōng, jiāotōng, tōngdào, tōng wǎng, tōngyòng

商

Seung` trade; business

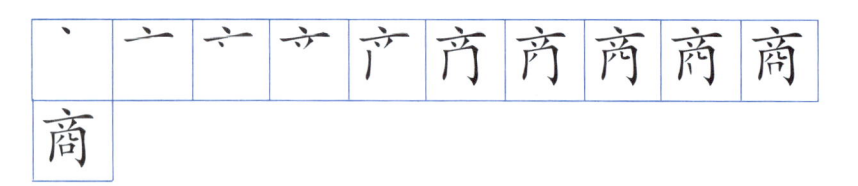

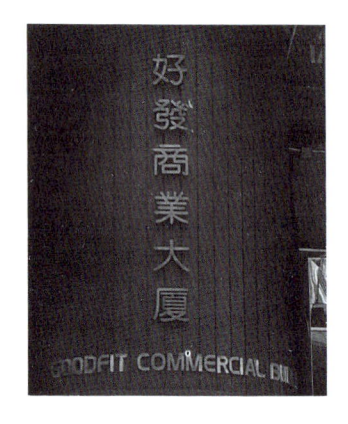

| 丶 | 宀 | 宀 | 宀 | 产 | 产 | 产 | 商 | 商 | 商 |

商

商務	seung` (trade)	mou— (matter)	executive, commercial (e.g. business class)
商鋪(鋪)	seung` (business)	pou— (store)	store
商店	seung` (business)	deem— (shop)	shop
商業中心	seung` (commerce)	yeep—	jung` (centre)	sam`	commercial center

Yale System : sèung, sèungmouh, sèungpou, sèungdim, sèungyihp jùngsàm

Lau System : seung¹, seung¹ mo⁶, seung¹ po³, seung¹ dim³, seung¹ yip⁶ jung¹ sam¹

Pinyin : shāng, shāng wù, shāng pù, shāngdiàn, shāngyè zhōngxīn

110

菜 　Choi– 　　dish of food; cuisine; vegetable

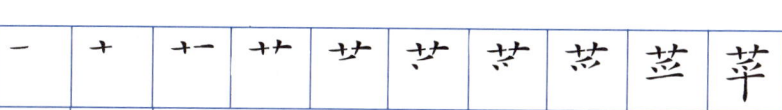

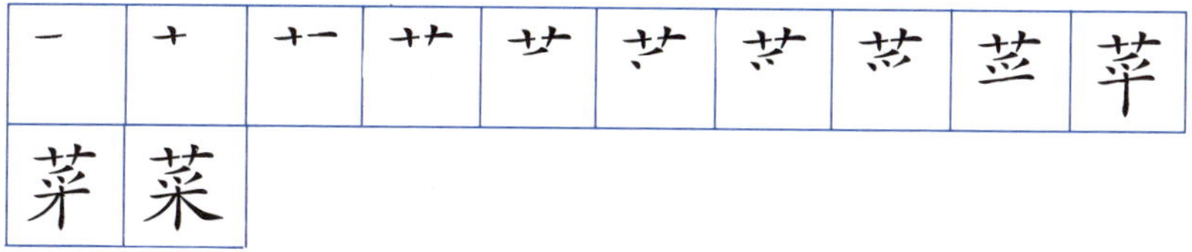

菜

| 一 | 十 | 十 | 艹 | 艹 | 艻 | 苧 | 苎 | 苙 | 苹 |

| 苹 | 菜 |

小菜	syu╱ (small)	choi– dish of food)	Chinese dishes
京菜	Ging╲ (Beijing)	choi– cuisine)	Beijing cuisine
粤菜	Yüt＿ (Cantonese)	choi– cuisine)	Cantonese cuisine
川菜	Chün╲ (Sichuan)	Choi– cuisine)	Sichuan cuisine

Yale System : choi, síuchoi, Gìngchoi, Yuhtchoi, Chyùnchoi

Lau System : choi[3], siu[2] choi[3], Ging[1] choi[3], Yut[6] choi[3], Chuen[1] Choi[3]

Pinyin : cài, xiǎocài, Jīngcài, Yuècài, Chuāncài

111

場 Cheung — spacious area

| 一 | 十 | 土 | 圵 | 圹 | 坦 | 坦 | 坦 | 埸 | 場 |

場 場

市場	see ╱ (market)	cheung ╲ (spacious area)	market
商場	seung ╲ (business)	cheung ╲ (spacious area)	shopping arcade
廣場	gwong ╱ (wide)	cheung ╲ (spacious area)	plaza (type of shopping centre)
機場	gei ╲ (aeroplane)	cheung ╲ (spacious area)	airport

Yale System : chèuhng, síhchèuhng, sèungchèuhng, gwóngchèuhng, gèichèuhng

Lau System : cheung⁴, si⁵ cheung⁴, seung¹ cheung⁴, gwong² cheung⁴, gei¹ cheung⁴

Pinyin : chǎng, shìchǎng, shāngchǎng, guǎngchǎng, jīchǎng

塲

| 港 | Gong⟋ | harbour | HONG KONG CEMETERY 香港墳場 |

| ` | `` | ⺡ | 氵 | 汁 | 汫 | 洪 | 浐 | 洪 | 浡 | 港 | 港 |

海港	hoi⟋ (sea)	gong⟋ (harbour)		harbour
港九	Gong⟋ (Hong Kong)	Gau⟋ Kowloon)		Hong Kong & Kowloon (shop sign)
中港城	Jung⟍ (China)	Gong⟋ Hong Kong	Sing⟍ City)	Hong Kong China City
港澳碼頭	Gong⟋ (Hong Kong)	Ou— Macau	Maa⟋ tau⟍ ferry)	Hong Kong-Macau Ferry Pier
省港澳	Saang⟋ (province	Gong⟋ Hong Kong	Ou— Macau)	Guangzhou-Hong Kong-Macau

Yale System : góng, hóigóng, Gónggáu, Jùnggóng Sìhng, Góng Ou Máhtàuh, Sáang Góng Ou

Lau System : gong², hoi² gong², Gong² gau², Jung¹ gong² Sing⁴, Gong² O³ Ma⁵ tau⁴, Saang² Gong² O³

Pinyin : gǎng, hǎigǎng, Gǎngjiǔ, Zhōnggǎng Chéng, Gǎng Ào Mǎtou, Shěng Gǎng Ào

113

街 Gaay⁻ street

丁 ノ ⺌ 彳 彳 扩 狆 徏 徏 徏 街 街 街

西洋菜街	Saiˋ (watercress)	yeungˋ	choi—	Gaay⁻ street)	Sai Yeung Choi Street (in Mongkok)
廟街	Myu_ (temple)		Gaay⁻ street)		Temple Street (in Kowloon)
上海街	Seung_ (on	hoi´ sea	Gaay⁻ street)		Shanghai Street (in Kowloon)
雲咸街	Wanˋ	haamˋ	Gaay⁻ (street)		Wyndham Street (on Hong Kong Island)

Rumsey Street 林士街

Yale System : gāai, Sàiyèungchoi Gāai, Miuh Gāai, Seuhnghói Gāai, Wàhnhàahm Gāai

Lau System : gaai¹⁰, Sai¹ yeung⁴ choi³ Gaai¹⁰, Miu⁶ Gaai¹⁰, Seung⁶ hoi² Gaai¹⁰, Wan⁴ haam⁴ Gaai¹⁰

Pinyin : jiē, Xīyángcaì Jiē, Miào Jiē, Shànghǎi Jiē, Yúnxián Jiē

等   Dang′   wait; class (grade)

SPECIAL CLASS: 2:30 p.m.-3:30 p.m. 特等房

ノ	⺁	⺌	⺮	⺮	⺮	⺮	笙	笙
等	等							

等候	dang′ (wait)	hau＿ (moment)	wait (part of traffic sign for 'No Waiting')
頭等	tau＼ (head)	dang′ (class)	first class (train, Starry Ferry)
二等	yee＿ (two)	dang′ (class)	second class
特等	dak＿ (special)	dang′ (class)	dress circle (cinema)

Yale System : dáng, dánghauh, tàuhdáng, yihdáng, dahkdáng
Lau System : dang², dang² hau⁶, tau⁴ dang², yi⁶ dang², dak⁶ dang²
Pinyin : děng, děnghòu, tóuděng, èrděng, těděng

115

新　　　San`　　　new

、	亠	亠	立	立	立	辛	辛	亲	新
新	新	新							

新力	San` (new)	lik ‾ (power)		Sony
新年	san` (new)	neen ` (year)		new year
新界	San` (new)	gaay ‾ (boundary)		New Territories
新世界	San` (new)	Sai ‾ (world)	gaay ‾ (boundary)	New World (Hotel, Centre, etc.)

Yale System : sàn, Sànlihk, sànnìhn, Sàn-gaai, Sànsaigaai

Lau System : san¹, San¹ lik⁶, san¹ nin⁴, San¹ gaai³, San¹ sai³ gaai³

Pinyin : xīn, Xīnlì, xīnnián, Xīnjiè, Xīnshìjiè

道   Dou‾   road

Middle Road 中間道

| 丶 | 丷 | 丷 | 厸 | 产 | 芐 | 首 | 首 | 首 | 首 |

| 道 | 道 | 道 |

隧道	seuy‾ (underground)	dou‾ road)		subway, tunnel
佐敦道	Jor /	deun‾	Dou‾ (road)	Jordan Road (in Kowloon)
彌敦道	Nei \	deun‾	Dou‾ (road)	Nathan Road (in Kowloon)
金鐘道	Gam‾ (gold	jung‾ bell	Dou‾ road)	Queensway (in Hong Kong)

Yale System   : douh, seuihdouh, Jódēun Douh, Nèihdēun Douh, Gāmjūng Douh

Lau System   : do⁶, sui⁶ do⁶, Joh² dun¹⁰ Do⁶, Nei⁴ Dun¹⁰ Do⁶, Gam¹⁰ jung¹⁰ Do⁶

Pinyin   : dào, suìdào, Zuǒdūn Dào, Mídūn Dào, Jīnzhōng Dào

117

電 Deenˍ electricity

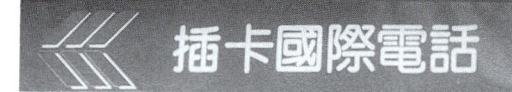

插卡國際電話

一	厂	戸	兩	丙	雨	雨	雨	雨	雫
雫	雷	電							

電話	deenˍ (electricity)	waa ´ word)	telephone
電視	deenˍ (electricty)	seeˍ sight)	television
電梯	deenˍ (electricity)	tai ` ladder)	esculator, lift
電車	deenˍ (electricty)	che ` car)	tram car
電腦	deenˍ (electric	nou ∕ brain)	computer

Yale System : dihn, dihnwá, dihnsih, dihntài, dihnchè, dihnnóuh

Lau System : din[6], din[6] wa[2], din[6] si[6], din[6] tai[1], din[6] che[1], din[6] no[5]

Pinyin : diàn, diànhuà, diànshì, diàntī, diànchē, diànnǎo

118

Hou—   number ; horn

号

80. DES VOEUX ROAD CENTRAL
德 輔 道 中 八 十 號

丶	口	口	吕	号	号'	号⸍	号⸍	号⸍
號	號	號						

二號	yee— (two)	hou— number)		number two
五號	ng ⸝ (five)	hou— number)		number five
六號	luk— (six)	hou— number)		number six
不准響號	Bat— (not	jeun ⸝ allow	heung ⸝ sound	hou— horn)	No sounding horns

---

Yale System   :   houh, yihhouh, n̄ghhouh, luhkhouh, bātjéun héung houh

Lau System   :   ho⁶, yi⁶ ho⁶, ng⁵ ho⁶, luk⁶ ho⁶, bat¹⁰ jun² heung² ho⁶

Pinyin   :   hào, èrhào, wǔhào, liùhào, bùzhǔn xiǎng hào

業 Yeep – trade

业

| 丶 | 丷 | 丷 | 业 | 业 | 业 | 业 | 业 | 业 | 业 |

| 業 | 業 | 業 |

SHANGHAI COMMERCIAL BANK LTD.

工業	gung` (work)	yeep_ (trade)	industry
商業	seung` (business)	yeep_ (trade)	commerce
專業	jün` (special)	yeep_ (trade)	We specialize in (shop sign)
營業中	ying` (engage in)	yeep_ (trade)	jung` (middle)	open for business (sign on shop doors)

Yale System : yihp, gùngyihp, sèungyihp, jyùnyihp, yìhngyihpjùng

Lau System : yip⁶, gung¹ yip⁶, seung¹ yip⁶, juen¹ yip⁶, ying⁴ yip⁶ jung¹

Pinyin : yè, gōngyè, shāngyè, zhuānyè, yíngyèzhōng

Yün ́ leisure place

新 立 本 幼 稚 園
New Foundation Kindergarten

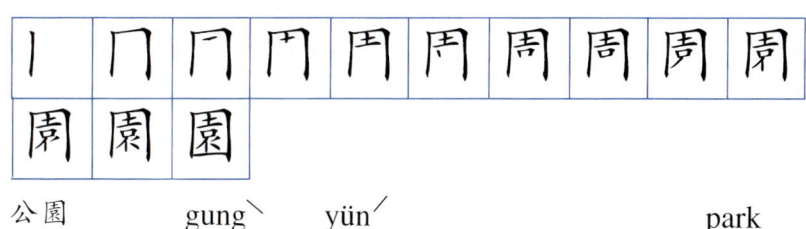

園　园

一	冂	冂	冂	冃	禺	禺	周	周

禺	園	園

公園	gung ˋ (public)	yün ́ leisure place)	park
花園	faa ˋ (flower)	yün ́ leisure place)	garden, residential estate
翠園	Cheuy — (green)	yün ́ leisure place)	Jade Garden (name of restaurant)
幼稚園	yau — (small)	jee — infant	yün ́ leisure place)	Kindergarten

---

Yale System　:　yún, gùngyún, fàyún, Cheuiyún, yaujihyún

Lau System　:　yuen², gung¹ yuen², fa¹ yuen², Chui³ yuen², yau³ ji⁶ yuen²

Pinyin　　　:　yuán, gōngyuán, huāyuán, Cuìyuán, yòuzhìyuán

裝　　Jong⁻　　wear, style
　　　　　　　(department store signs)

| ⼂ | 十 | ナ | 爿 | 爿一 | 爿土 | 壯 | 壯 | 壯 | 裝 |

| 裝 | 裝 | 裝 |

女裝　　neuy╱　　jong⁻　　ladies' wear
　　　　(female)　(wear)

男裝　　naam╲　　jong⁻　　mens' wear
　　　　(male)　　(wear)

時裝　　see╲　　jong⁻　　fashion
　　　　(time)　　(wear)

童裝　　tung╲　　jong⁻　　children's wear
　　　　(children)　(wear)

Yale System　:　jōng, néuih jōng, nàahm jōng, sìhjōng, tùhng jōng

Lau System　:　jong[10], nui[5] jong[10], naam[4] jong[10], si[4] jong[10], tung[4] jong[10]

Pinyin　　　:　zhuāng, nǔzhuāng, nánzhuāng, shízhuāng, tóngzhuāng

會

Wooy´, Wooy_ meeting; association

会

丿	亻	人	亼	合	佥	侖	會	會	會
會	會	會							

商會　　seung` wooy´　　　　　　　　trade union
　　　　(business association)

大會堂　Daay_ wooy´ tong`　　　　　City Hall
　　　　(big　meeting　hall)

青年會　Ching` neen` wooy´　　　　Y.M.C.A.
　　　　(young year association)

夜總會　ye_ jung´ wooy´　　　　　　night club
　　　　(night general meeting)

Yale System : wúi, sèung wúi, Daaihwúitòhng, Chìngnìhnwúi, yehjúngwúi

Lau System : wooi², seung¹ wooi², Daai⁶ wooi² tong⁴, Ching¹ nin⁴ wui², ye⁶ jung² wui²

Pinyin : huì, shānghuì, Dàhuìtáng, Qīngniánhuì, yèzǒnghuì

飾 　Sik⁻　　decoration

饰

| 丿 | 𠂉 | ㇱ | 㐅 | 今 | 今 | 𠆢 | 食 | 飠 | 飠 |

| 飲 | 飭 | 飾 |

金飾　gam⁻ 　　sik⁻ 　　　　gold and jewellery (shop sign)
　　　(gold)　(decoration)

首飾　sau´ 　　sik⁻ 　　　　jewellery
　　　(head)　(decoration)

裝飾　jong⁻ 　sik⁻ 　　　　interior decoration
　　　(put)　 (decoration)

燈飾　dang⁻ 　sik⁻ 　　　　lighting
　　　(light)　(decoration)

Yale System　:　sīk, gāmsīk, sáusīk, jōngīk, dāngsīk
Lau System　:　sik¹⁰, gam¹⁰ sik¹⁰, sau² sik¹⁰, jong¹⁰ sik¹⁰, dang¹⁰ sik¹⁰
Pinyin　　　:　shì, jīnshì, shǒushi, zhuāngshì, dēngshì

禁　　　Gam−　　prohibit

| 一 | 十 | 才 | 木 | 木 | 村 | 材 | 林 | 林 | 埜 |

| 埜 | 禁 | 禁 |

禁止	gam−(prohibit)	jíestop)		prohibited (road sign)
禁區	gam−(prohibit)	keuy`area)		Security Area
禁煙區	gam−(prohibit)	yeen−smoke	keuy`area)	no-smoking section
嚴禁標貼	Yim`(	gam−prohibit	biu`	teep−posting)	No posting, no billsticking

Yale System : gam, gam jí, gam kèui, gam yīn kèui, Yìhm gam bìutip

Lau System : gam³, gam³ ji², gam³ kui¹, gam³ yin¹⁰ kui¹, Yim⁴ gam³ biu¹ tip³

Pinyin : jìn, jìnzhǐ, jìnqū, jìn yān qū, Yán jìn biāotiē

125

傳 Chünˋ   pass; call; spread

传

| 丿 | 亻 | 仁 | 仨 | 伫 | 伫 | 佰 | 俥 | 俥 | 傳 |
| 傳 | 傳 | 傳 |

傳呼機   chünˋ (pass)   fooˋ call   geiˋ machine)   Pager

傳真   chünˋ (pass)   janˋ authentic)   Fax

傳播   chünˋ (spread)   bor– send)   Mass media (shop sign, production house)

Yale System : chyùhn, chyùhn fù gèi, chyùhnjàn, chyùhnbo

Lau System : chuen⁴, chùen⁴ foo¹ gei¹, chuen⁴ jan¹, chuen⁴ boh³

Pinyin : chuán, chuánhū jī, chuánzhēn, chuánbō

碼 Maaˊ ferry; pier

码

| 一 | 厂 | 丆 | 石 | 石 | 石˙ | 石˭ | 石˫ | 石⼿ | 碼 |

| 碼 | 碼 | 碼 | 碼 |

STAR FERRY CONCOURSE SITTING OUT AREA
天星碼頭廣場 休憩處

天星碼頭	Teenˋ (sky)	singˋ star	Maaˊ	tauˋ pier	Star Ferry Pier
港澳碼頭	Gongˊ (Hong Kong)	Ou— Macau	Maaˊ	tauˋ pier	Hong Kong Macau Ferry Pier
港外線碼頭	Gongˊ (Hong Kong)	ngoiˍ outside	seen— line	Maaˊ tauˋ pier	Outlying Islands Ferry Pier

Yale System: mǎh, Tìnsìng Mǎhtàuh, Góng-Ou Mǎhtàuh, Góngngoih sin Máhtàuh

Lau System : ma⁵, Tin¹ sing¹ Ma⁵ tau⁴, Gong² O³ Ma⁵ tau⁴, Gong¹² ngoi⁶ sin³ Ma⁵ tau⁴

Pinyin   : mǎ, Tiānxīng Mǎtou, Gǎng-Ào Mǎtou, Gǎngwài xiàn Mǎtou

127

樓　　Lau ˋ　　building
楼

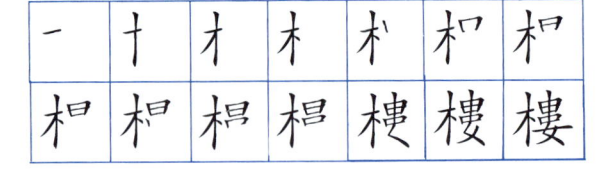

| 一 | 十 | 才 | 木 | 木 | 朾 | 柯 |
| 柯 | 柯 | 柺 | 椙 | 樓 | 樓 | 樓 |

樓上	lau ˋ (building)	seung ˉ (up)		upstairs
樓下	lau ˋ (building)	haa ˉ (down)		downstairs
酒樓	jau ˊ (wine)	lau ˋ (building)		Chinese restaurant
茶樓	chaa ˋ (tea)	lau ˋ (building)		teahouse
寫字樓	se ˊ (write)	ji ˉ (character)	lau ˋ (building)	office

Sea View Restaurant (海景酒樓)

Yale System : làuh, làuhseuhng, làuhhah, jáulàuh, chàhlàuh, séjihlàuh

Lau System : lau⁴, lau⁴ seung⁶, lau⁴ ha⁶, jau² lau⁴, cha⁴ lau⁴, se² ji⁶ lau⁴

Pinyin　　； lóu, lóushàng, lóuxià, jiǔlóu, chálóu, xiězìlóu

| 銀 | Ngan ˋ | silver |

| ノ | 𠂉 | ㇉ | 𠂉 | 午 | 余 | 余 | 金 | 鈩 | 鈩 |
| 鈤 | 鈤 | 銀 | 銀 |

中國銀行	Jung ˋ (Middle	gwok ˉ Kingdom	Ngan ˋ silver	hong ˋ firm)	Bank of China
恆生銀行	Hang ˋ (persistent	Sang ˋ growth	Ngan ˋ silver	hong ˋ firm)	Hang Seng Bank
美國銀行	Mei ／ (Beautiful	gwok ˉ country	Ngan ˋ silver	hong ˋ firm)	Bank of America
匯豐銀行	Wooy ˍ (China	fung ˉ Hong Kong	Ngan ˋ City)	hong ˋ	Hongkong Bank

Yale System : ngàhn, Jùnggwok Ngàhnhòhng, Hàhngsàng Ngàhnhòhng, Méihgwok Ngàhnhòhng, Wuihfūng Ngàhnhòhng

Lau System : ngan[4], Jung[1] gwok[3] Ngan[4] hong[4], Hang[4] sang[1] Ngan[4] hong[4], Mei[5] gwok[3] Ngan[4] hong[4], Wooi[6] fung[10] Ngan[4] hong[4]

Pinyin   : yín, Zhōngguó Yínháng, Héngshēng Yínháng, Měiguó Yíháng, Huìfēng Yínháng

Ching ˊ   please

請

| 丶 | 二 | 三 | 三 | 言 | 言 | 言 | 言 | 詰 |

| 詰 | 請 | 請 | 請 | 請 |

請候	chíng (please)	hau (wait)			Please wait!
請讓座	chíng (please)	yeung (give up)	jor (seat)		Please give your seat! (in bus)
請勿吸煙	chíng (please)	mat (do not)	kap (suck)	yeen (smoke)	Please don't smoke! (in bus)
請勿進入	chíng (please)	mat (do not)	jeun (enter)	yap (enter)	Please don't enter!

Yale System : chíng, chíng hauh, chíng yeuhng joh, chíng maht Kāpyīn, chíng maht jeunyahp

Lau System : ching², ching² hau⁶, ching² yeung⁶ joh⁶, ching² mat⁶ kap¹⁰ yin¹⁰, ching² mat⁶ jun³ yap⁶

Pinyin   : qǐng, qǐng hòu, qǐng ràng zuò, qǐng wù xīyān, qǐng wù jìnrù

賣　　Maay˗　　sell (alternative
卖　　　　　　of 售 Sau˗)

男仕精品大特賣
MEN'S ACCESSORIES BARGAIN

一	十	士	士	吉	吉	吉	吉	青
青	青	賣	賣	賣				

拍賣　　paak˗　　maay˗　　　　　　auction
　　　　(strike　(sell)

高賣　　gou`　　maay˗　　　　　　shoplifting (part of store sign for 'No Shoplifting)
　　　　(high　(sell)

買賣　　maay´　maay˗　　　　　　business (part of shop name)
　　　　(buy　　(sell)

大平賣　daay˗　peng`　　maay˗　　big sale
　　　　(big　　cheap　　sell)

Yale System : Maaih, paakmaaih, gòumaaih, máaihmaaih, daaih pèhngmaaih

Lau System : Maai⁶, paak³ maai⁶, go¹ maai⁶, maai⁵ maai⁶, daai⁶ peng⁴ maai⁶

Pinyin : Mài, pāimài, gāomaì, măimai, dà píngmài

價	gaa –	price
		(on shop signs)

价

ノ	亻	亻	仁	伊	侢	俌	俌	價
價	價	價	價	價				

平價	peng ╲ (inexpensive)	gaa – price)	low price
半價	boon – (half)	gaa – price)	half price
特價	dak _ (special)	gaa – price)	special price
大減價	daay _ (big)	gaam ╱ reduction	gaa – price)	big sale

Yale System : ga, pèhng ga, bun ga, dahk ga, daaih gáamga

Lau System : ga³, peng⁴ ga³, boon³ ga³, dak⁶ ga³, daai⁶ gaam² ga³

Pinyin : jià, píng jià, bàn jià, tè jià, dà jiǎnjià

Geiˋ machine

機 机

一	十	才	木	朾	朾	桦	桦	桦	桦
桦	桦	桦	機	機	機				

相機　　seung ˊ　　gei ˋ　　　　　　camera
　　　　(photo)　　(machine)

遊戲機　yau ˋ　　hei −　　gei ˋ　　Computer game centre
　　　　(　game)　　　　　(machine)

洗衣機　sai ˊ　　yee ˋ　　gei ˋ　　washing machine
　　　　(wash)　(clothes)　(machine)

電視機　deen −　　see −　　gei ˋ　　television set
　　　　(electricity)　(sight)　(machine)

Yale System : gèi, séunggèi, yàuhheigei, sáiyìgèi, dihnsihgèi

Lau System : gei¹, seung² gei¹, yau⁴ hei³ gei¹, sai² yi¹ gei¹, din⁶ si⁶ gei¹

Pinyin : jī, xiàngjī, yóuxìjī, xǐyījī, diànshìjī

學　　Hok— learn

学

| ` | ⺊ | F | F | F' | F' | 臼 | 臼 | 臼ㄱ | 臼ㄱ |

| 臼ㄱ | 臼ㄱ | 與 | 學 | 學 | 學 |

學校　hok— （learn）　haaw— (school)　school

小學　syu´ (small)　hok— (school)　primary school

中學　jung` (middle)　hok— (school)　secondary school

大學　daay— (big)　hok— (school)　university

Yale System : hohk, hohkhaauh, síuhohk, jùnghohk, daaihhohk

Lau System : hok⁶, hok⁶ haau⁶, siu² hok⁶, jung¹ hok⁶, daai⁶ hok⁶

Pinyin : xué, xuéxiào, xiǎoxué, zhōngxué, dàxué

險　　Heemˊ　　risk; risky

险

ˊ	ˋ	阝	阝ʹ	阝ᐞ	阝ᐞ	阝ᐞ	阝ᐞ	阝ᐞ
險	險	險	險	險	險			

保險	bouˊ (protect)	heemˊ risk)	insurance
火險	forˊ (fire)	beemˊ risk)	fire insurance
水險	seuyˊ (water)	heemˊ risk)	water insurance
危險	ngaiˋ (danger)	heemˊ risk)	danger, dangerous (on road sign)

Yale System　:　hím, bóuhím, fóhím, séui hím, ngàihhím

Lau System　:　him², bo² him², foh² him², sui² him², ngai⁴ him²

Pinyin　　　:　xiǎn, báoxiǎn, huǒxiǎn, shuǐxiǎn, wēixiǎn

135

餐

Chaan⁻ meal

飡

丶	ト	ㅏ	ㅗ	夕	歺	歺	歺	癸	癸
餐	餐	餐	餐	餐	餐				

自助餐	jee⁻ (self)	jor⁻ help	chaan⁻ meal)	buffet
套餐	tou⁻ (set)	chaan⁻ meal)		set meal
快餐店	faay⁻ (fast)	chaan⁻ meal	deem⁻ store)	fast food store
茶餐廳	chaaˋ (tea	chaan⁻	teng⁻ restaurant)	Hong Kong style cafe

Yale System : chāan, jihjoh chāan, tou chāan, faai chāan dim, chàh chāan tēng

Lau System : chaan¹⁰, ji⁶ joh⁶ chaan¹⁰, to³ chaan¹⁰, faai³ chaan¹⁰ dim³, cha⁴ chaan¹⁰ teng¹⁰

Pinyin   : cān, zìzhù cān, tào cān, kuài cān diàn, chá cān tīng

	Goon´	building
館		
舘		

中央圖書館
oon Central Library

| ノ | 𠆢 | 𠂉 | 今 | 今 | 今 | 𩙿 | 𩙿 | 𩙿 | 𩙿 |
| 飣 | 飣 | 節 | 飭 | 館 | 館 | | | | |

圖書館	tou﹨ (picture	sü book	goon´ building)	library
博物館	bok — (general	mat — object	goon´ building)	museum
菜館	choy — (dish	goon´ building)		restaurant
餐館	chaan — (meal	goon´ building)		(Western) restaurant

Yale System : gwún, tòuhsyù gwún, bokmaht gwún, choi gwún, chāan gwún

Lau System : goon², to⁴ sue¹ goon², bok³ mat⁶ goon², choi³ goon², chaan¹⁰ goon²

Pinyin   : guǎn, túshū guǎn, bówù guǎn, cài guǎn, cān guǎn

| 龍 | Lung丶 | dragon |

Kowloon East 九龍東

| 丶 | 亠 | 产 | 㐰 | 立 | 产 | 产 | 亨 | 亨 |
| 产 | 产 | 产 | 龍 | 龍 | 龍 | 龍 | | |

九龍	Gau╱(nine)	lung丶(dragon)		Kowloon
九龍城	Gau╱(nine)	lung丶(dragon)	Sing丶(city)	Kowloon City
九龍塘	Gau╱(nine)	lung丶(dragon)	Tong丶(pool)	Kowloon Tong (MTR and KCR Stations)
龍島	Lung丶(dragon)	dou╱(island)		Lucullus

Yale System : lùhng, Gáulùhng, Gáulùhng Sìhng, Gáulùhng Tòhng, Lùhngdóu

Lau System : lung⁴, Gau² lung⁴, Gau² lung⁴ Sing⁴, Gau² lung⁴ Tong⁴, Lung⁴ do²

Pinyin : lóng, Jiǔlóng, Jiǔlóng Chéng, Jiǔlóng Táng, Lóngdǎo

醫 Yeeˋ cure

医

| 一 | 𠂇 | 𠂉 | 匚 | 医 | 医 | 医 | 殹 | 殹 |

| 殹 | 殹 | 殹 | 殹 | 殹 | 殹 | 殹 | 醫 |

醫生	yeeˋ (cure)	sangˉ (person)		doctor
港中醫院	gong´ (Hong Kong)	jungˋ China	yeeˋ hospital)	yün´	Hong Kong Central Hospital
中醫	Jungˋ (Chinese)	yeeˋ (cure)		doctor trained in Chinese medicine (on signs)
西醫	saiˋ (west)	yeeˋ (cure)		doctor trained in Western medicine (on signs)

Yale System : yì, yìsāng, Góng Jùng Yìyún, Jùngyì, sàiyì

Lau System : yi¹, yi¹ sang¹⁰, Gong² Jung¹ Yi¹ yuen², Jung¹ yi¹, sai¹ yi¹

Pinyin : yī, yīsheng, Gáng Zhōng Yīyuàn, Zhōngyī, xīyī

139

Meenˍ Noodle

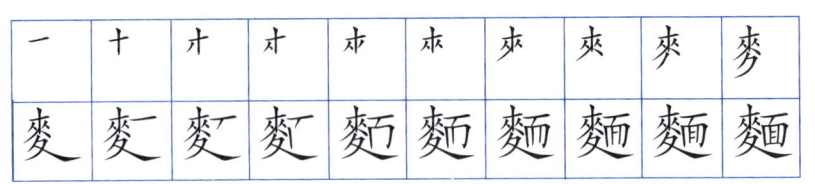

麵

面

一	十	艹	𠂉	朩	來	夾	夾	夾	麥

| 麥 | 麨 | 麨 | 麨 | 麵 | 麵 | 麵 | 麵 | 麵 | 麵 |

粥麵　　juk¯　　　meenˍ　　　　　　　congee and noodle
　　　　(congee　 noodle)

麵包　　meenˍ　　baau¯　　　　　　　bread
　　　　(noodle　 bun)

雲吞麵　wan﹅　　tan¯　　　meenˍ　　wonton noodle
　　　　(　　wonton　　　　noodle)

杯麵　　booy¯　　meenˍ　　　　　　　cup noodle
　　　　(cup　　 noodle)

"麵", the conventional word, is originally written as "麵". It has now been recognized as a full form, especially occuring on shop signs. The simplified form is "面" which also means "the face" as in "面孔"

Yale System : mihn, jūkmihn, mihnbāau, wàhntàn mihn, buīmihn

Lau System : min⁶, juk¹⁰ min⁶, min⁶ baau¹⁰, wan⁴ tan¹⁰ min⁶, booi¹⁰ min⁶

Pinyin : miàn, zhōumiàn, miànbāo, húntun miàn, bēi miàn

麵

灣

Waan⁻ bay

湾

灣仔	Waan⁻ (bay)	jai´ (small)		Wan chai (HK Island)
淺水灣	Cheen´ (Shallow)	seuy´ water	Waan⁻ bay)	Repulse Bay (HK Island)
深水灣	Sam` (deep)	seuy´ water	Waan⁻ bay)	Deep Water Bay (HK Island)
銅鑼灣	Tung` (bronze)	lor` gong	Waan⁻ bay)	Causeway Bay (HK Island)

Yale System : wāan, Wāanjái, Chínséui Wāan, Sàmséui Wāan, Tùhnglòh Wāan

Lau System : waan¹⁰, Waan¹⁰ jai², Chin² sui² Waan¹⁰, Sam¹ sui² Waan¹⁰, Tung⁴ loh⁴ Waan¹⁰

Pinyin : wān, Wānzǎi, Qiǎnshuǐ Wān, Shēnshuǐ Wān, Tóngluó Wān

Numbers

0	零	lingˋ		10	十	sap–	
1	一	yat¯		11	十一	sap–	yat¯
2	二(兩)	yee–	(leungˊ)	22	二十二	yee–	sap– yee–
3	三	saamˋ		33	三十三	saamˋ	sap– saamˋ
4	四	sei–		44	四十四	sei–	sap– sei–
5	五	ngˊ		55	五十五	ngˊ	sap– ngˊ
6	六	luk–		66	六十六	luk–	sap– luk–
7	七	chat¯		77	七十七	chat¯	sap– chat¯
8	八	baatˊ		88	八十八	baatˊ	sap– baatˊ
9	九	gauˊ		99	九十九	gauˊ	sap– gauˊ

Numbers on Minibus and Market Price Signs

一個元	$1.50	gor−	boon−		一元	$1.10	gor−	yat−	
三元二元	$2.00	leung⁄	man¯		二元	$2.20	leung⁄	gor−	yee−
二個元	$2.50	leung⁄	gor−	boon−		三元	$3.30	saam`	gor−	saam`
三元三元	$3.00	saam`	man¯		十四元	$14.00	sap−	sei−	man¯

143

價錢					價錢				
三元 四毫	$3.40	saam`	gor-	sei-	二十 五元	$25.00	yee_	sap_	ng/ man-
四元	$4.00	sei-	man-		三十 六元	$36.00	saam`	sap_	luk_ man-
四元 六毫	$4.60	sei-	gor-	luk_	四十 七元	$47.00	sei-	sap_	chat- man-
五元	$5.00	ng/	man-		五十 八元	$58.00	ng/	sap_	baat- man-
六元 七毫	$6.70	luk_	gor-	chat-	六十 九元	$69.00	luk_	sap_	gau/ man-
七元 八毫	$7.80	chat-	gor-	baat-	七十 一元	$71.00	chat-	sap_	yat- man-
八元 九毫	$8.90	baat-	gor-	gau/	八十 二元	$82.00	baat-	sap_	yee_ man-
九元	$9.00	gau/	man-		九十 三元	$93.00	gau/	sap_	saam` man-
十元	$10.00	sap_	man-		一百 元	$100.00	yat-	baak-	man-

Major Buildings

Admiralty Centre	海富中心	Hoi´ foo— Jung` sam`
Airport Terminal Bldg	機場大廈	Gei` cheung` Daay_ haa_
Alexandra House	歷山大廈	Lik_ saan` Daay_ haa_
Ashley Mansion	雅士洋樓	Ngaa´ see` Yeung` lau´
Asian House	熙信大廈	Hei` seun— Daay_ haa_
Bank Centre	銀行中心	Ngan` hong` Jung` sam`
Bank of America Bldg	美國銀行大廈	Mei´ gwok— Ngan` hong` Daay_ haa_
Bank of America Tower	美國銀行中心	Mei´ gwok— Ngan` hong` Jung` sam`
Bank of China Bldg	中國銀行大廈	Jung` gwok— Ngan` hong` Daay_ haa_
Bank of East Asia Bldg	東亞銀行大廈	Dung` Aa— Ngan` hong` Daay_ haa_
Capitol Centre	京華中心	Ging` waa´ Jung` sam`
Causeway Bay Centre	銅鑼灣中心	Tung` lor` Waan` Jung` sam`
Central Bldg	中建大廈	Jung` geen— Daay_ haa_
Central Government Offices	政府合署	Jing— foo´ Hap_ chü´
China Bldg	華人行	Waa` yan` Hong´
China Travel Bldg	中旅大廈	Jung` leuy´ Daay_ haa_
Central Plaza	中環廣場	Jung` waan` Gwong´ cheung`
China Resources Bldg	華潤大廈	Waa` yun— Daay_ haa_

145

Chung King Mansion	重慶大廈	Chung↘	hing–	Daay_	haa_	
City Hall	大會堂	Daay_	wooy_	Tong↘		
City Plaza	太古城中心	Taay–	gwoo´	Sing↘	Jung↘	sam↘
Dragon Seed Bldg	龍子行	Lung↘	Jee´	Hong´		
Elizabeth House	伊利莎伯大廈	Yee↘	lei_	saa↘	baak–	Daay_ haa_
Entertainment Building	娛樂行	Yü↘	Lok_	Hong´		
Exchange Square	交易廣場	Gaaw↘	yik_	Gwong´	cheung↘	
Gloucester Tower	告羅士打大廈	Gou–	lor↘	see–	daa´	Daay_ haa_
HK & Shanghai Bank Bldg	匯豐銀行大廈	Wooy↘	fung‾	Ngan_	Hong↘	Daay_ haa_
HK Club Bldg	香港會大廈	Heung↘	gong´	Wooy↘	Daay_	haa_
Harbour Centre	海港中心	Hoi´	gong´	Jung↘	sam↘	
Harbour City	海港城	Hoi´	gong´	Sing↘		
Hennessy Centre	興利中心	Hing↘	lei_	Jung↘	sam↘	
Hong Kong Arts Centre	藝術中心	Ngai↘	seut_	Jung↘	sam↘	
HK Convention & Exhibition Centre	香港會議展覽中心	Heung↘	gong´	Wooy_	yee´	
		Jin´	laam´	Jung↘	sam↘	
International Finance Centre	國際金融中心	Gwok–	jai–	Gam↘	yung↘	Jung↘ sam↘
Jardine House	怡和大廈	Yee↘	wor´	Daay_	haa_	
Landmark	置地廣場	Jee–	dei_	Gwong´	cheung↘	
Leighton Centre	禮頓中心	Lai	deun_	Jung↘	sam↘	
Lippo Centre	力寶中心	Lik_	bou´	Jung↘	sam↘	

New World Centre	新世界中心	San`	Sai−	gaay_	Jung`	sam`
New World Tower	新世界大廈	San`	Sai−	gaay_	Daay`	haa_
Ocean Centre	海洋中心	Hoi´	yeung`	Jung`	sam`	
Ocean Terminal	海運大廈	Hoi´	wan_	Daay`	Haa_	
Pacific Place	太古廣場	Taay_	gwoo´	Gwong´	cheung`	
Peak Tower	凌峰閣	Ling`	fung`	Gok_		
Pedder Bldg	畢打行	Bat−	daa`	Hong´		
Prince's Bldg	太子大廈	Taai−	jee´	Daay`	Haa_	
Queensway Plaza	金鐘廊	Gam−	jung−	Long`		
Shun Tak Centre	信德中心	Seun−	Dak−	Jung`	sam`	
Sino Plaza	信和廣場	Seun−	wor´	Gwong´	cheung`	
Star House	星光行	Sing`	gwong`	Hong´		
Sunning Plaza	新寧大廈	San`	ning`	Daay`	Haa_	
Supreme Court	最高法院	Jeuy−	gou−	Faat−	yün´	
Swire House	太古大廈	Taay−	gwoo´	Daay`	haa_	
The Centre	中環中心	Jung`	waan`	Jung`	saam`	
Times Square	時代廣場	See`	doi_	Gwong´	cheung`	
Watson's Estate	屈臣氏大廈	Wat−	san`	see´	Daay_	haa_
World Finance Centre	環球金融中心	Waan`	Kau`	Gam−	yung`	Jung` sam`
World Trade Centre	世界貿易中心	Sai−	gaay−	Mau_	yik_	Jung` sam`
World Wide House	環球大廈	Waan`	kau`	Daay_	haa_	

147

Hotels

Ambassador Hotel	國賓酒店	Gwok–	ban\	Jau/	deem–		
Ascot Apartment Hotel	雅閣酒店	Ngaa/	gok–	Jau/	deem–		
Astor Hotel	蘭宮酒店	Laan\	gung\	Jau/	deem–		
Atrium, The	曦暹軒	Hei\	cheem–	Heen‾			
Bangkok Royal Hotel	曼谷貴賓酒店	Maan_	guk‾	Gwai–	ban\	Jau/	deem–
BP International	龍堡國際	Lung\	Bou/	Gwok–	jai–	Jau/	deem–
Caravelle Hotel	帆船酒店	Faan\	sün\	Jau/	deem–		
Century Hong Kong Hotel	世紀香港酒店	Sai–	gei/	Heung\	Gong/	Jau/	deem–
Charterhouse Hotel	利景酒店	Lei_	ging/	Jau/	deem–		
China Harbour View Hotel	中華海景酒店	Jung\	waa\	Hoi/	ging/	Jau/	deem–
China Merchants Hotel	華商酒店	Waa\	Seung\	Jau/	deem–		
Chung Hing Hotel	中興酒店	Jung\	Hing\	Jau/	deem–		
City Garden Hotel	城市花園酒店	Sing\	si/	fa\	yün/	Jau/	deem–
Concourse Hotel	京港酒店	Ging\	Gong/	Jau/	deem–		
Conrad International Hotel	港麗酒店	Gong/	Lai\	Jau/	deem–		
Eastin Valley Hotel	東豪酒店	Dung\	Hou/	Jau/	deem–		
Eaton Hotel	逸東酒店	Yat_	dung\	Jau/	deem–		
Empire Hotel	皇悅酒店	Wong\	yüt_	Jau/	deem–		

Evergeen Hotel	萬年青酒店	Maan_	ninˋ	chingˋ	Jau´	deem–	
Excelsior Hotel	怡東酒店	Yeeˋ	dungˋ	Jau´	deem–		
First Hotel	第一酒店	Dai_	yat¯	Jau´	deem–		
Fortuna Hotel	富都酒店	Foo–	douˋ	Jau´	deem–		
Furama Hotel	富麗華酒店	Foo–	lai–	waaˋ	Jau´	deem–	
Galaxie Hotel	嘉來酒店	Gaaˋ	loiˋ	Jau´	deem–		
Gold Coast Hotel	黃金海岸酒店	Wongˋ	gamˋ	Hoi´	ngon_	Jau´	deem–
Grand Hotel	格蘭酒店	Gaak–	laanˋ	Jau´	deem–		
Grand Hyatt Hotel	君悅香港酒店	Gwanˋ	yüt_	Heungˋ	Gong´	Jau´	deem–
Grand Plaza Hotel	康蘭酒店	Hongˋ	laanˋ	Jau´	deem–		
Grand Stanford Harbour View	海景嘉福酒店	Hoi´	ging´	Gaˋ	fuk¯	Jau´	deem–
Grand Tower Hotel (in Kln.)	雅蘭酒店	Ngaa´	laanˋ	Jau´	deem–		
Guangdong Hotel	粵海酒店	Yüt_	hoi´	Jau´	deem–		
Harbour Plaza	海逸酒店	Hoi´	yat_	Jau´	deem–		
Harbour Hotel	華國酒店	Waaˋ	gwok–	Jau´	deem–		
Harbour View International House	灣景國際賓館	Waanˋ	ging´	Gwok–	jai–	Banˋ	gwoon´
Hillview Hotel	山景酒店	Saanˋ	ging´	Jau´	deem–		
Holiday Inn Golden Mile Hotel	金域假日酒店	Gam¯	wikˋ	Gaa¯	yat–	Jau´	deem–
Hong Kong Hotel	香港酒店	Heungˋ	gong´	Jau´	deem–		
Hyatt Regency Hotel	凱悅酒店	Hoi´	yüt–	Jau´	deem–		
Imperial Hotel	帝國酒店	Dai¯	gwok–	Jau´	deem–		

149

International Hotel	國際酒店	Gwok− jai− Jau╱ deem−
Island Shangri-la Hotel	港島香格里拉酒店	Gong╱ dou╲ Heung− gaak− lei╱ laai╲ Jau╱ deem−
Jade Hotel	翡翠酒店	Fei╲ cheuy− Jau╱ deem−
Kimberley Hotel	君怡酒店	Gwan╲ yee╲ Jau╱ deem−
King's Hotel	高雅酒店	Gou╲ ngaa╱ Jau╱ deem−
Kowloon Hotel	九龍酒店	Gau╲ lung╲ Jau╱ deem−
Kowloon Panda Hotel	九龍悅東酒店	Gau╲ lung╲ Yüt− dung╲ Jau╱ deem−
Luk Kwok Hotel	六國酒店	Luk− Gwok− Jau╱ deem−
Majestic Hotel	大華酒店	Daay− waa╲ Jau╱ deem−
Mandarin Oriental Hotel	文華酒店	Man╲ waa╲ Jau╱ deem−
Marco Polo Hotel	馬哥孛羅酒店	Maa╱ gor╲ boot− lor╲ Jau╱ deem−
Marriott Hotel	萬豪酒店	Maan╲ hou╲ Jau╱ deem−
Metropole Hotel	京華酒店	Ging╲ waa╲ Jau╱ deem−
Miramar Hotel	美麗華酒店	Mei╲ lai− waa╲ Jau╱ deem−
Nathan Hotel	彌敦酒店	Nei╲ deun− Jau╱ deem−
New Astor Hotel	新雅圖酒店	San╲ ngaa╱ tou╲ Jau╱ deem−
New Cathay Hotel	新國泰酒店	San╲ Gwok− Taay− Jau╱ deem−
New Harbour Hotel	星港酒店	Sing╲ gong╱ Jau╱ deem−
New World Hotel	新世界酒店	San╲ Sai− gaay╲ Jau╱ deem−
New World Harbour View Hotel	新世界海景酒店	San╲ Sai− gaay╲ Hoi╲ ging╱ Jau╱ deem−
Newton Hotel	麗東酒店	Lai− dung╲ Jau╱ deem−

English	Chinese	Romanization
Nikko Hotel	日航酒店	Yat̲ hongˎ Jau´ deem–
Park Kowloon Hotel	百樂酒店	Baak– lok̲ Jau´ deem–
Park Lane Hotel	柏寧酒店	Paak– lingˎ Jau´ deem–
Parkside	柏舍	Paak– Se–
Pearl Seaview Hotel	明珠海景酒店	Mingˎ jü` Hoi´ ging´ Jau´ deem–
Peninsula Hotel	半島酒店	Boon– dou´ Jau´ deem–
Prince Hotel	太子酒店	Taay– jee´ Jau´ deem–
Prudential Hotel	恆豐酒店	Hangˎ fung` Jau´ deem–
Ramada Kowloon	九龍華美達酒店	Gau´ lungˎ Waaˎ mei/ daat̲ Jau´ deem–
Hong Kong Renaissance	華美達麗新酒店	Waaˎ mei/ daat̲ Lai̲ san` Jau´ deem–
Regal Hong Kong Hotel	富豪香港酒店	Foo– houˎ Heung` Gong´ Jau´ deem–
Regal Airport Hotel	富豪機場酒店	Foo– houˎ Gei` cheungˎ Jau´ deem–
Regal Kowloon Hotel	富豪酒店	Foo– houˎ Jau´ deem–
Regal Plaza Hotel	富豪廣場酒店	Foo– houˎ Gwong´ cheungˎ Jau´ deem–
Regal Riverside Hotel	麗豪酒店	Lai̲ houˎ Jau´ deem–
Regent Hotel	麗晶酒店	Lai̲ jing` Jau´ deem–
Ritz Hotel	樂斯酒店	Lok̲ see` Jau´ deem–
Royal Garden Hotel	帝苑酒店	Dai– yün´ Jau´ deem–
Royal Pacific Hotel	皇家太平洋酒店	Wongˎ gaa` Taay– pingˎ Yeungˎ Jau´ deem–
Royal Park Hotel	帝都酒店	Dai– dou` Jau´ deem–
San Diego Hotel	聖地牙哥酒店	Sing– dei̲ ngaaˎ gor` Jau´ deem–

151

Shamrock Hotel	新樂酒店	San` lok_ Jau´ deem⁻
Shangri-La Hotel	香格里拉酒店	Heung` gaak⁻ lei´ laay` Jau´ deem⁻
Sheraton Hotel	喜來登酒店	Hei´ loi` dang⁻ Jau´ deem⁻
Silvermine Beach Hotel	銀鑛灣酒店	Ngan` Kong_ Waan⁻ Jau´ deem⁻
Sonth China Hotel	粤華酒店	Yüt_ Waa` Jau´ deem⁻
South Pacific Hotel	南洋酒店	Naam` yeung` Jau´ deem⁻
Stanford Hillview Hotel	仕德福山景酒店	See_ dak⁻ fuk⁻ Saan` ging´ Jau´ deem⁻
Stanford Hotel	仕德福酒店	See_ dak⁻ fuk⁻ Jau´ deem⁻
The Wesley	衛蘭軒	Wai` laan` Heen⁻
The Wharney Hotel	香港華美酒店	Heung` gong´ Waa` mei´ Jau´ daam⁻
Warwick Hotel Cheung Chau	長洲華威酒店	Cheung` Jau⁻ Waa` Wai` Jau´ deem⁻
Windsor Hotel	温莎酒店	Wan` saa` Jau´ deem⁻
YMCA (European)	西人青年會	San` yan` Ching` neen` Wooy´
YMCA Harbour View International House	青年會灣景國際賓館	Ching` neen` Wooy´ Waan⁻ ging´ Gwok⁻ jai⁻ Ban` gwoon´
YMCA International House	青年會國際賓館	Ching` neen` Wooy´ Gwok⁻ jai⁻ Ban` gwoon´
(YWCA) Garden View International House	花園國際賓館	Faa` yün` Gwok⁻ jai⁻ Ban` gwoon´

Major Hospitals

Baptist Hospital	浸信會醫院	Jam– seun– Wooy´ Yee` yün´
Caritas Medical Centre	明愛醫院	Ming` Oi– Yee` yün´
Graham Hospital	葛量洪醫院	Got– leung_ hung` Yee` yün´
Hong Kong Adventist Hospital	港安醫院	Gong´ On` Yee` yün´
Hong Kong Central Hospital	港中分科醫院	Gong´ Jung– Fan` for– Yee` yün´
HK Sanatorium & Hospital	養和醫院	Yeung´ wor` Yee` yün´
Kwong Wah Hospital	廣華醫院	Gwong´ waa` Yee` yün´
Matilda & War Memorial Hospital	明德醫院	Ming` dak– Yee` yün´
Pamela Youde Nethesole Eastern Hospital	尤德夫人拿打素東區醫院	Yau` dak– Foo` yan` Naa` daa´ Sou– Dung` keuy´ Yee` Yün´
Pok Oi Hospital	博愛醫院	Bok– Oi– Yee` yün´
Prince of Wales Hospital	威爾斯醫院	Wai` yee´ see` Yee` yün´
Princess Margaret Hospital	瑪嘉烈醫院	Maa´ gaa` leet_ Yee` yün´
Queen Elizabeth Hospital	伊利沙伯醫院	Yee` lei_ saa` baak– Yee` yün´
Queen Mary Hospital	瑪麗醫院	Maa´ Lai` Yee` yün´
St. Paul's Hospital	聖保祿醫院	Sing– bou´ luk_ Yee` yün´
St. Teresa's Hospital	聖德肋撒醫院	Sing– dak– lak_ saat– Yee` yün´
Tang Shiu Kin Hospital	鄧肇堅醫院	Dang_ syu` geen` Yee` yün´

United Christian Hospital 聯合醫院 Lün、 hap＿ Yee` yün´

Major Banks

English	Chinese	Romanization
American Express Bank	美國運通銀行	Mei／ gwok- wan_ tung＼ Ngan＼ hong＼
Bangkok Bank	盤谷銀行	Poon＼ guk- Ngan＼ hong＼
Bank of America	美國銀行	Mei／ gwok- Ngan＼ hong＼
Bank of China	中國銀行	Jung＼ gwok- Ngan＼ hong＼
The Bank of East Asia	東亞銀行	Dung＼ aa- Ngan＼ hong＼
Bank of Tokyo	東京銀行	Dung＼ ging／ Ngan＼ hong＼
Banque National de Paris	法國巴黎銀行	Faat- gwok- Baa＼ lai＼ Ngan＼ hong＼
Belgian Bank	華比銀行	Waa＼ bei／ Ngan＼ Hong＼
Chase Manhattan Bank	美國大通銀行	Mei／ gwok- Daay- tung＼ Ngan＼ hong＼
Citibank	萬國寶通銀行	Maan- gwok- Bou／ tung＼ Ngan＼ hong＼
The Commercial Bank of Hong Kong	香港商業銀行	Heung＼ gong／ Seung＼ yeep- Ngan＼ hong＼
Dao Heng Bank	道亨銀行	Douh- hang／ Ngan＼ hong＼
First Pacific Bank	第一太平銀行	Dai- Yat- Taay- Ping＼ Ngan＼ hong＼
Hang Seng Bank Ltd.	恆生銀行	Hang＼ Sang＼ Ngan＼ hong＼
The Hongkong Bank	匯豐銀行	Wooy- fung／ Ngan＼ Hong＼
International Bank of Asia	港基國際銀行	Gong／ gei＼ Gwok- jai- Ngan＼ hong＼
The Ka Wa Bank	嘉華銀行	Gaa＼ waa＼ Ngan＼ hong＼
Kwong On Bank	廣安銀行	Gwong／ on＼ Ngan＼ hong＼

155

Liu Chong Hing Bank	廖創興銀行	Liu₋ chong₋ hingˋ Nganˎ hongˎ
Nanyang Commercial Bank	南洋商業銀行	Naamˎ yeungˎ Seungˋ yeep₋ Nganˎ hongˎ
Overseas Trust Bank	海外信託銀行	Hoi´ ngoi₋ Seun₋ tok₋ Nganˎ hongˎ
Po Sang Bank	寶生銀行	Bou´ sangˋ Nganˎ hongˎ
The Sanwa Bank	三和銀行	Saamˋ worˎ Nganˎ hongˎ
Security Pacific Asian Bank	太平洋亞洲銀行	Taay₋ Pingˎ Yeungˋ Aa₋ jauˋ Nganˎ hongˎ
Sin Hua Bank	新華銀行	Sanˋ Waaˎ Nganˎ hongˎ
Standard Chartered Bank	渣打銀行	Jaaˋ daa´ Nganˎ hongˎ
Wing Hang Bank	永亨銀行	Wing´ hangˋ Nganˎ hongˎ

Streets and Roads

Hong Kong Island

Aberdeen Main Road	香港仔大道	Heungˋ gongˋ jai´ Daayˍ douˍ
Arsenal Street	軍器廠街	Gwanˋ hei- chong´ Gaay-
Bank Street	銀行街	Nganˋ hongˋ Gaay-
Bisney Road	碧荔道	Bik- laiˍ Douˍ
Black's Link	布力徑	Bouˋ likˍ Ging-
Blue Pool Road	藍塘道	Laamˋ tongˋ Douˍ
Bonham Road	般咸道	Boonˋ haamˋ Douˍ
Borrett Road	波老道	Borˋ lou´ Douˍ
Bowen Road	寶雲道	Bou´ wanˋ Douˍ
Braemar Hill Road	寶馬山道	Bou´ maa´ Saanˋ Douˍ
Broadwood Road	樂活道	Lokˍ wootˍ Douˍ
Broom Road	蟠龍道	Poonˋ lungˋ Douˍ
Caine Road	堅道	Geenˋ Dou´
Caroline Hill Road	加路連山道	Gaaˋ louˍ leenˋ Saanˋ Douˍ
Castle Road	衛城道	Waiˍ singˋ Douˍ
Chater Road	遮打道	Jeˋ daa´ Douˍ
Chun Fai Terrace	春暉臺	Cheunˋ faiˋ Toiˋ

157

Chung Hom Kok Road	春磡角道	Jung ˋ	ham –	gok –	Dou ˍ	
Cleverly Street	急庇利街	Gap ˉ	bei ˋ	lei ˍ	Gaay ˉ	
Club Street	會所街	Wooy ˍ	Sor ˊ	Gaay ˉ		
Conduit Road	干德道	Gon ˋ	dak –	Dou ˍ		
Connaught Road Central	干諾道中	Gon ˋ	lok –	Dou ˍ	jung ˋ	
D'Aguilar Street	德己立街	Dak ˉ	gei ˊ	lap ˍ	Gaay ˉ	
Deep Water Bay Road	深水灣道	Sam ˋ	seuy ˊ	Waan –	Dou ˍ	
Des Voeux Road Central	德輔道中	Dak ˉ	foo ˉ	Dou –	Jung ˋ	
Garden Road	花園道	Faa ˋ	yün ˋ	Dou ˍ		
Gilman's Bazaar	機利文新街	Gei ˋ	lei –	man ˋ	san ˋ	Gaay ˉ
Gilman's Street	機利文街	Gei ˋ	lei –	man ˋ	Gaay ˉ	
Gloucester Road	告士打道	Gou –	see ˍ	daa ˊ	Dou ˍ	
Hennessy Road	軒尼詩道	Heen ˋ	nei ˋ	see ˋ	Dou ˍ	
Hollywood Road	荷李活道	Hor ˋ	lei ˊ	Woot ˍ	Dou ˍ	
Hospital Road	醫院道	Yee ˋ	yün ˊ	Dou ˍ		
Hysan Road	希慎道	Hei ˋ	san –	Dou ˍ		
Ice House Street	雪廠街	Süt –	chong ˊ	Gaay ˉ		
Jaffe Road	謝斐道	Je ˍ	fei ˋ	Dou ˍ		
Kennedy Road	堅尼地道	Geen ˋ	nei ˋ	dei –	Dou ˍ	
King's Road	英皇道	Ying ˋ	wong ˋ	Dou ˍ		
Lan Kwai Fong	蘭桂坊	Laan ˋ	Gwai –	Fong ˉ		

Macdonnell Road	麥當奴道	Mak˗	dongˋ	louˋ	Dou˗	
Magazine Gap Road	馬己仙峽道	Maaˊ	geiˊ	seenˋ	haap˳	Dou˗
May Road	梅道	Mooy˳	dou˗			
Mosque Street	嚤囉廟街	Mor˳	lor˳	myuˊ	Gaay˗	
Mount Austin Road	柯士甸山道	Or˳	See˗	deen˳	Saan˳	Dou˗
Mount Butler Drive	畢拉山道	Bat˗	laay˳	Saan˳	Dou˗	
Mount Davis Road	摩星嶺道	Mor˳	Sing˳	lengˊ	Dou˗	
Murray Road	美利道	Meiˊ	lei˗	Dou˗		
Nam Fung Road	南風道	Naam˳	fung˳	Dou˗		
Old Peak Road	舊山頂道	Gau˗	Saan˳	dengˊ	Dou˗	
On Lan Street	安蘭街	On˳	laan˳	Gaay˗		
Pak Pat Shan Road	白筆山道	Baak˗	bat˗	Saan˳	Dou˗	
Park Road	柏道	Paak˗	dou˗			
Paterson Street	百德新街	Baak˗	dak˗	San˳	Gaay˗	
Peak Road	山頂道	Saan˳	dengˊ	Dou˗		
Peddar Street	畢打街	Bat˗	daaˊ	Gaay˗		
Percival Street	波斯富街	Bor˳	see˳	foo˗	Gaay˗	
Perkins Road	白建時道	Baak˗	geen˗	see˳	Dou˗	
Po Shan Road	寶珊道	Bouˊ	saan˳	Dou˗		
Pokfulam Road	薄扶林道	Bok˗	foo˳	lam˳	Dou˗	
Queen's Road Central	皇后大道中	Wong˳	hou˗	daay˗	Dou˗	jung˳

Queensway	金鐘道	Gam¯ jung¯ Dou_
Repulse Bay Road	淺水灣道	Cheen´ Seuy´ Waan¯ Dou_
Robinson Road	羅便臣道	Lor、 been_ san、 Dou_
Sa Wan Drive	沙灣徑	Saa` Waan¯ Ging–
Sandy Bay Road	大口環道	Daay_ hau´ Waan、 Dou_
Sassoon Road	沙宣道	Saa` sün¯ Dou_
Seymour Road	西摩道	Sai` mor、 Dou_
Shan Kwong Road	山光道	Saan` gwong´ Dou_
Shek O Road	石澳道	Sek_ ou – Dou_
Shiu Fai Terrace	肇輝臺	Syu_ fai` Toi´
Shouson Hill Road	壽山村道	Sau_ Saan` Chün` Dou_
Sing Woo Road	成和道	Sing´ wor、 Dou_
South Bay Road	南灣道	Naam、 waan¯ Dou_
Stanley Main Street	赤柱大街	Chek – chü´ Daay_ Gaay–
Stubbs Road	司徒拔道	See` tou´ bat_ Dou_
Sunning Road	新寧道	San` ning´ Dou_
Tai Hang Road	大坑道	Daay_ haang` Dou_
Tai Tam Reservoir Road	大潭水塘道	Daay_ taam、 Seuy´ tong、 Dou_
Tai Tam Road	大潭道	Daay_ taam、 Dou_
Tin Hau Temple Road	天后廟道	Teen` hau_ myu´ Dou_
Upper Albert Road	上亞厘畢道	Seung_ aa – lei、 bat¯ Dou_

Ventris Road	雲地利道	Wan ˋ	dei ˍ	lei ˊ	Dou ˍ	
Village Road	山村道	Saan ˋ	chün ˋ	Dou ˍ		
Wan Chai Road	灣仔道	Waan ˉ	jai ˊ	Dou ˍ		
Wang Fung Terrace	宏豐臺	Wang ˋ	fung ˋ	Toi ˋ		
Wong Nai Chung Gap Road	黃泥涌峽道	Wong ˋ	nai ˋ	chung ˋ	haap ˍ	Dou ˍ
Wong Nai Chung Road	黃泥涌道	Wong ˋ	nai ˋ	chung ˋ	Dou ˍ	
Wood Road	活道	Woot ˍ	Dou ˍ			
Wyndham Street	雲咸街	Wan ˋ	haam ˋ	Gaay ˉ		

Kowloon

Argyle St.	亞皆老街	Aa ˉ	gaay ˋ	lou ˊ	Gaay ˉ	
Ashley Rd.	亞士厘道	Aa ˉ	see ˍ	lei ˋ	Dou ˍ	
Austin Rd.	柯士甸道	Or ˋ	see ˍ	deen ˋ	Dou ˍ	
Beacon Hill Rd.	筆架山道	Bat ˉ	gaa ˊ	Saan ˋ	Dou ˍ	
Boundary St.	界限街	Gaay ˉ	haan ˍ	Gaay ˉ		
Broadcast Drive	廣播道	Gwong ˊ	bor ˍ	Dou ˍ		
Canton Rd.	廣東道	Gwong ˊ	dung ˋ	Dou ˍ		
Carnavan Rd.	加拿芬道	Gaa ˋ	naa ˍ	fan ˋ	Dou ˍ	
Castle Peak Rd.	青山道	Ching ˋ	Saan ˋ	Dou ˍ		
Chatham Rd.	漆咸道	Chat ˉ	haam ˋ	Dou ˍ		
Clear Water Bay Rd.	清水灣道	Ching ˋ	seuy ˊ	Waan ˉ	Dou ˍ	

161

Cox's Rd.	覺士道	Gok˗	see˗	Dou˗			
Cumberland Rd.	金巴倫道	Gam`	baa`	leun`	Dou˗		
Gascoigne Rd.	加士居道	Gaa`	see˗	geuy`	Dou˗		
Hankow Rd.	漢口道	Hon`	hau´	Dou˗			
Hillwood Rd.	山林道	Saan`	lam`	Dou˗			
Homantin Hill Rd.	何文田山道	Hor`	man`	teen`	Saan`	Dou˗	
Homantin St.	何文田街	Hor`	man`	teen`	Gaay˗		
Hop Yat Rd.	合一道	Hap˗	yat˗	Dou˗			
Jordan Rd.	佐敦道	Jor`	deun`	Dou˗			
Junk Bay Rd.	將軍澳道	Jeung`	gwan`	ou˗	Dou˗		
Kimberley Rd.	金巴利道	Gam`	baa`	lei˗	Dou˗		
King's Park Rise	京士柏道	Ging`	see˗	paak˗	Dou˗		
Ko Shan Rd.	高山道	Gou`	Saan`	Dou˗			
Kowloon City Rd.	九龍城道	Gau´	lung`	Sing`	Dou˗		
Kwai Chung Rd.	葵涌道	Kwai`	chung`	Dou˗			
La Salle Rd.	喇沙利道	laa˗	Saa`	lei˗	Dou˗		
Lai Chi Kok Rd.	荔枝角道	lai˗	jee`	gok˗	Dou˗		
Lei Yue Mun Rd.	鯉魚門道	lei´	yü`	moon`	Dou˗		
Lion Rock Rd.	獅子石道	See`	jee´	sek`	Dou˗		
Lion Rock Tunnel Rd.	獅子山隧道公路	see`	jee´	Saan`	Seuy˗	dou˗	Gung` lou˗
Lock Rd.	樂道	Lok˗	Dou˗				

Man Fuk Rd.	文福道	Man ˋ	Fuk ˉ	Dou ˍ		
Middle Rd.	中間道	Jung ˋ	gaan ˋ	Dou ˍ		
Mody Rd.	麽地道	Mor ˋ	dei ˋ	Dou ˍ		
Nathan Rd.	彌敦道	Nei ˋ	deun ˋ	Dou ˍ		
Peking Rd.	北京道	Bak ˉ	ging ˋ	Dou ˍ		
Perth St.	巴富街	Baa ˋ	foo ˉ	Gaay ˉ		
Prince Edward Rd.	太子道	Taay ˋ	jee ˊ	Dou ˍ		
Princess Margaret Rd.	公主道	Gung ˋ	jü ˊ	Dou ˍ		
Salisbury Rd.	梳士巴利道	Sor ˋ	see ˍ	baa ˋ	lei ˋ	Dou ˍ
Shanghai St.	上海街	Seung ˍ	hoi ˊ	Gaay ˉ		
Temple St.	廟街	Myu ˊ	Gaay ˉ			
Tin Kwong Rd.	天光道	Teen ˋ	gwong ˋ	Dou ˍ		
Waterloo Rd.	窩打老道	Wor ˋ	daa ˊ	lou ˊ	Dou ˍ	
Wong Tai Sin Rd.	黃大仙道	Wong ˋ	daay ˍ	seen ˋ	Dou ˍ	

MTR Stations 地鐵站 (Dei‿ teet¯ Jaam‿)

Island Line	港島線	Gong´	dou´	seen⁻
Chai Wan	柴灣	Chaay‿	Waan⁻	
Heng Fa Chuen	杏花村	Hang_	faa﹅	Chün⁻
Shaukeiwan	筲箕灣	Saaw﹅	gei﹅	waan⁻
Sai Wan Ho	西灣河	Sai﹅	waan⁻	hor´
Tai Koo	太古	Taay-	gwoo´	
Quarry Bay	鰂魚涌	Jak⁻	yü﹅	chung⁻
North Point	北角	Bak⁻	gok⁻	
Fortress Hill	炮台山	Paaw-	toi﹅	Saan﹅
Tin Hau	天后	Teen﹅	hau_	
Causeway Bay	銅鑼灣	Tung﹅	lor﹅	Waan⁻
Wan Chai	灣仔	Waan⁻	jai´	
Admiralty	金鐘	Gam⁻	jung⁻	
Central	中環	Jung﹅	waan﹅	
Sheung Wan	上環	Seung_	waan﹅	
Kwun Tong Line	官塘線	Gwoon﹅	tong﹅	seen-
Yaumatei	油麻地	Yau﹅	maa﹅	dei´
Mongkok	旺角	Wong_	gok-	

Prince Edward	太子	Taay-	jee´	
Shek Kip Mei	石硤尾	Sek_	geep-	mei´
Kowloon Tong	九龍塘	Gau´	lungˎ	tongˎ
Lok Fu	樂富	Lok_	foo-	
Wong Tai Sin	黃大仙	Wongˎ	daay_	seen˛
Diamond Hill	鑽石山	Jün-	sek_	Saan˛
Choi Hung	彩虹	Choi´	hungˎ	
Kowloon Bay	九龍灣	Gau´	lungˎ	Waan-
Ngau Tau Kok	牛頭角	Ngauˎ	tauˎ	gok-
Kwun Tong	觀塘	Gwoon˛	tongˎ	
Lam Tin	藍田	Laamˎ	teenˎ	
Tsuen Wan Line	荃灣線	Chünˎ	Waan-	Seen-
Central	中環	Jung˛	waanˎ	
Admiralty	金鐘	Gam-	jung-	
Tsim Sha Tsui	尖沙咀	Jeem˛	Saa˛	jeuy´
Jordon	佐敦	Jor´	deun˛	
Yaumatei	油麻地	Yauˎ	maaˎ	dei´
Mongkok	旺角	Wong_	gok-	
Prince Edward	太子	Taay-	jee´	
Sham Shui Po	深水埗	Sam˛	Seuy´	bou´
Cheung Sha Wan	長沙灣	Cheungˎ	Saa˛	Waanˎ

English	Chinese	Cantonese
Lai Chi Kok	荔枝角	Lai₋ jeeˋ gok⁻
Mei Foo	美孚	Mei´ Fooˋ
Lai King	荔景	Lai₋ ging´
Kwai Fong	葵芳	Kwaiˋ fongˋ
Kwai Hing	葵興	Kwaiˋ hingˋ
Tai Wo Hau	大窩口	Daay₋ worˋ hau´
Tsuen Wan	荃灣	Chünˋ waan₋
Tung Chung Line	東涌線	Dungˋ chung´ Seen⁻
Central Station	中環站	Jungˋ waan´ Jaam₋
Kowloon Station	九龍站	Gau´ lungˋ Jaam₋
Olympic Station	奧運站	Ou⁻ wan₋ Jaam₋
Lai King Station	荔景站	Lai₋ ging´ Jaam₋
Tsing Yi Station	青衣站	Chingˋ yeeˋ Jaam₋
Tung Chung Station	東涌站	Dungˋ chung´ Jaam₋
Airport Express	機場快線	Geiˋ cheungˋ Faay⁻ seen⁻
Hong Kong Station	香港站	Heungˋ gong´ Jaam₋
Kowloon Station	九龍站	Gau´ lungˋ Jaam₋
Tsing Yi Station	青衣站	Chingˋ yeeˋ Jaam₋
Airport Station	機場站	Geiˋ cheungˋ Jaam₋

KCR Stations 九廣鐵路站 (Gau´ Gwong´ Teet- lou_ Jaam_)

Kowloon (i.e. Hunghom)	九龍	Gau´	lung`	
Mong Kok	旺角	Wong_	gok-	
Kowloon Tong	九龍塘	Gau´	lung`	Tong`
Tai Wai	大圍	Daay_	Wai_	
Shatin	沙田	Saa`	teen`	
Fo Tan	火炭	For´	taan-	
University	大學	Daay_	hok_	
Tai Po Market	大埔墟	Daay_	bou–	heuy`
Tai Wo	太和	Taay-	Wor`	
Fanling	粉嶺	Fan´	leng´	
Sheung Shui	上水	Seung_	Seuy´	
Lo Wu	羅湖	Lor`	Woo`	

Cinemas, Theatres and Cultural Venues

Academic Community Hall	大專會堂	Daay˯	yün˴	Wooy˯	tong˴				
Arts Centre	藝術中心	Ngai˴	seut˗	Jung˴	sam˴				
Astor Classics Cinema	普慶戲院	Pou˷	hing—	Hei–	yün˷				
Broadway Cinema	百老匯戲院	Baak–	lou˷	wooi˷	Hei–	yün˷			
Chinachem Cinema	華懋戲院	Waa˴	mau—	Hei–	yün˷				
Cine Art House	影藝戲院	Ying˷	ngai˴	Hei–	yün˷				
City Hall	大會堂	Daay˯	wooy˯	tong˴					
Columbia Classics Cinema	新華戲院	San˴	waa˷	Hei–	yün˷				
Dynamax	無限地帶	Mou˴	haan—	Dei˯	daay–				
Empress Cinema	凱聲戲院	Hoi˷	sing˴	Hei–	yün˷				
Golden Harvest	嘉禾戲院	Gaa˴	wor˴	Hei–	yün˷				
Golden Lee Theatre	利舞臺	Lei˯	mou˷	Toi˴					
Harbour City Cinema	海城戲院	Hoi˷	sing˴	Hei–	yün˷				
Hong Kong Academy for Performing Arts	香港演藝學院	Heung˴	gong˷	Yeen˷	ngai—	Hok˯	yün˷		
Hong Kong Coliseum	紅磡體育館	Hung˴	ham—	Tai˷	yuk—	Gwoon˷			
Hong Kong Cultural Centre	香港文化中心	Heung˴	gong˷	Man˴	Faa˷	Jung˴	sam˴		
New Imperial Theatre	京都戲院	Ging˴	dou˴	Hei–	yün˷				

168

Isis Theatre	新都戲院	San`	dou`	Hei–	yün´			
Jade Theatre	翡翠戲院	Fei`	cheuy–	Hei–	yün´			
Ko Shan Theatre	高山劇院	Gou`	saan`	Kek_	yün´			
Liberty Theatre	快樂戲院	Faay–	lok_	Hei–	yün´			
London Theatre	倫敦戲院	Leun`	deun–	Hei–	yün´			
Majestic Cinema	大華戲院	Daay_	waa`	Hei–	yün´			
Miramar Cinema	美麗華戲院	Mei´	lai_	waa`	Hei–	yün´		
Park Theatre	百樂戲院	Baak–	lok–	Hei–	yün´			
Pearl Theatre	明珠戲院	Ming`	jü`	Hei–	yün´			
President Theatre	總統戲院	Jung´	tung´	Hei–	yün´			
Queen's Theatre	皇后戲院	Wong`	hau–	Hei–	yün´			
Queen Elizabeth Stadium	伊利沙伯體育館	Yee`	lei–	saa`	baak–	Tai´	yuk–	Gwoon´
Rex Theatre	文華戲院	Man`	waa`	Hei–	yün´			
Royal Theatre	麗聲戲院	Lai–	sing`	Hei–	yün´			
Sai Wan Ho Civic Centre	西灣河文娛中心	Sai`	waan–	hor´	Man`	yü´	Jung`	sam`
Sha Tin Town Hall	沙田大會堂	Saa`	teen`	Daay–	wooy–	tong`		
Sheung Wan Civic Centre	上環文娛中心	Seung–	waan`	Man`	yü´	Jung`	sam`	
Silvercord Cinema	新港戲院	San`	gong´	Hei–	yün´			
Space Museum	太空館	Taay–	hung`	Gwoon´				
State Theatre	皇都戲院	Wong`	dou`	Hei–	yün´			
Sunbeam Theatre	新光戲院	San`	gwong`	Hei–	yün´			

Tsuen Wan Town Hall	荃灣大會堂	Chünˋ	waan¯	Daay–	wooy–	tongˋ	
UA Queensway Cinema	UA金鐘戲院	YÜ¯	Ei¯	Gam¯	jung¯	Hei–	yün´
UA Times Square	UA時代廣場	YÜ¯	Ei¯	Seeˋ	doi_	Gwong´	cheungˋ
Washington Theatre	華盛頓戲院	Waaˋ	sing_	deun–	Hei–	yün´	
Yuen Long Town Hall	元朗大會堂	Yünˋ	long´	Daay–	wooy–	tongˋ	

Tourist and Sightseeing Places

Hong Kong Island

Aberdeen	香港仔	Heungˋ gong´ jai´
Bank of China Tower	中銀大廈	Jungˋ nganˋ Daay_ haa_
Cat Street (antique market)	摩囉街	Morˋ Lorˋ Gaay¯
Edinburgh Place	愛丁堡廣場	Oi_ dingˋ bou´ Gwong´ Cheungˋ
Hong Kong Museum of Art (inside City Hall)	香港藝術館	Heungˋ gong´ Ngai_ Seut_ Gwoon´
Hong Kong Park	香港公園	Heungˋ gong´ Gungˋ yün´
Jumbo Floating Restaurant	珍寶海鮮舫	Janˋ bou´ Hoi´ Seenˋ Fong´
Law Uk Folk Museum	羅屋民族館	Lorˋ Uk¯ Manˋ Juk_ Gwoon´
Man Mo Temple	文武廟	Manˋ mou´ Myu´
Museum of Tea Ware (inside Hong Kong Park)	茶具文物館	Chaaˋ geui_ Manˋ mat_ Gwoon´
Ocean Park	海洋公園	Hoi´ yeungˋ Gungˋ yün´
Planetarium	科學館	Forˋ hok_ Gwoon´
Repulse Bay and Tin Hau Temple	淺水灣及天后廟	Cheen´ seuy´ Waan¯ kap_ Teenˋ hau_ Myu´
St John's Cathedral	聖若翰教堂	Sing¯ yeuk_ hon_ Gaaw¯ tongˋ

171

Statue Square	皇后像廣場	Wong\	hou_	Jeung_	Gwong/	cheung\
Stanley Market	赤柱街市	Chek-	chü/	Gaay\	see/
The Peak	山頂	Saan\	deng/
Tiger Balm Garden	虎豹別墅	Foo/	paaw-	Beet_	seuy/
Western Market	西港城	Sai\	Gong/	Sing\
Zoological and Botanical Gardens	動植物公園	Dung_	jik_	mat_	Gung\	yün\

Outlying Islands

Cheung Chau	長洲	Cheung\	Jau\
Hong Kong International Airport	香港國際機場	Heung/	gong/	Gwok-	jai-	Gei\	cheung\
Lamma Island	南丫島	Naam/	aa\	Dou/
Po Lin Monastery, Lantau Island	寶蓮寺, 大嶼山	Bou/	Leen\	Jee/,	Daay_	yü\	Saan\

Kowloon

Bird Market Streetname: (Hong Lok Street)	雀仔街	Jeuk-	jai/	Gaay-
Chi Lin Nunnery	志蓮淨院	Jee-	lin\	Jing_	yün/
Clocktower	鐘樓	Jung-	lau\
Hong Kong Museum of History (inside Kowloon Park)	香港博物館	Heung\	gong/	Bok-	mat_	Gwoon/

Jade Market	玉器市場	Yuk‑ hei‑ See´ cheung`
Kowloon Mosque	九龍清真寺	Gou´ lung` Ching` Jan` jee´
Kowloon Park	九龍公園	Gau´ lung` Gung` yün´
Kowloon Walled City Park	九龍寨城公園	Gau´ lung` jaai‑ Sing` Gung` yün´
Lai Chi Kok Amusement Park	荔園	Lai‑ yün´
Li Cheng Uk Museum and Han Tomb	李鄭屋古墓	Lei´ jeng‑ uk‑ Goo´ mou‑
Ocean Terminal	海運中心	Hoi´ wan‑ Jung` sam`
Space Museum	太空館	Taay‑ hung` Gwoon´
Temple Street	廟街	Myu´ Gaay‑
Tung Choi Street	通菜街	Tung` choi‑ Gaay‑
Wong Tai Sin Temple	黃大仙廟	Wong` daay‑ seen` myu´

New Territories

Amah Rock (Shatin)	望夫石	Mong‑ foo` Sek‑
Che Kung Temple (Shatin)	車公廟	Che` gung` Myu´
Ching Chung Kwun Temple (Tuen Mun)	青松觀	Ching` Chung` Gwoon‑
Chinese University	中文大學	Jung` man` Daay‑ hok‑
Clearwater Bay (Sai Kung)	清水灣	Ching` seuy´ Waan`
Hebe Haven (Sai Kung)	白沙灣	Baak‑ saa` Waan`

Sam Tung Uk Museum (Tsuen wan)	三棟屋博物館	Saamˋ	dung˗	Uk˗	Bok˗	mat˗	Gwoon´
Tai Po Railway Museum (Tai Po)	大埔火車博物館	Daay˗	bou˗	Bok˗	mat˗	Gwoon´	
Ten Thousand Buddha Monastery (Shatin)	萬佛寺	Maan˗	fat˗	Jee´			
Tsing Ma Bridge	青馬大橋	Chingˋ	Ma´	Daay˗	kyuˋ		
Yuen Yuen Institute	圓玄學院	Yünˋ	yün´	Hok˗	yün´		
Western Monastery (Tsuen Wan)	西方寺	Saiˋ	fongˋ	Jee´			

Some Common Surnames

		Yale	*Pinyin*
Au	歐、區	Auˋ	Ōu
Au Yeung	歐陽	Auˋ yeungˎ	Ōu yáng
But	畢	Bat_	Bì
Che	車	Cheˋ	Chē
Chai	柴	Chaayˎ	Chái
Chan	陳	Chanˎ	Chén
Cheng	鄭	Jeng_	Zhèng
Cheung	張	Jeungˋ	Zhāng
Chin	錢	Chinˎ	Qián
Chiu	趙	Jyu_	Zhào
Cho	曹	Chouˎ	Cáo
Choi	蔡	Choi–	Cài
Chow	周、鄒	Jauˋ	Zhōu ; Zōu
Chu	朱	Jüˋ	Zhū
Chui	徐、崔	Cheuyˎ ; Cheuyˋ	Xú ; Cuī
Chung	鍾	Jungˋ	Zhòng
Fan	范	Faan_	Fàn

Fok	霍	Fok⁻	Huō
Fu	符	Fooˋ	Fú
Fung	馮	Fungˋ	Féng
Ho	何	Horˋ	Hé
Hon	韓	Honˋ	Hán
Hung	洪、孔	Hungˋ ; Hung´	Hóng ; Kǒng
Kam	金、甘	Gamˋ	Jīn ; Gān
Keung	姜	Geungˋ	Jiāng
Ko	高	Gouˋ	Gāo
Koo	顧	Goo⁻	Gù
Kong	江	Gongˋ	Jiāng
Ku	古	Gwoo´	Gǔ
Kwan	關	Gwaanˋ	Guān
Kwok	郭	Gok⁻	Guō
Kwong	鄺	Kong⁻	Kuàng
Lai	黎	Laiˋ	Lí
Lam	林	Lamˋ	Lín
Lau	劉	Lauˋ	Liú
Law	羅	Lorˋ	Luó
Lee/Li	李、利	Lei´ ; Lei⁻	Lǐ ; Lì
Leung	梁	Leungˋ	Liáng

Liu	廖	Lyu_	Liào
Lo	盧	Lou、	Lú
Lu	魯	Lou╱	Lǔ
Luk	陸	Luk_	Lù
Lui	呂	Leuy╱	Lǚ
Ma	馬	Maa╱	Mǎ
Mak	麥	Mak_	Mài
Mo	毛	Mou、	Máo
Mok	莫	Mok_	Mò
Ng	吳、伍	Ng、; Ng╱	Wú ; Wǔ
Pak	白	Baak_	Bái
Pang	彭	Paang、	Péng
Pao	包	Baaw、	Bāo
Poon	潘	Poon、	Pān
Shiu	邵	Syu_	Shào
So	蘇	Sou、	Sū
Szeto	司徒	See` tou、	Sī tú
Suen	孫	Sün`	Sūn
Sze	施	See`	Shī
Tam	譚	Taam、	Tán
Tang	鄧	Dang_	Dèng

Tin	田	Teen、	Tián
Ting	丁	Ding、	Dīng
To	杜	Dou—	Dù
Tong	唐、湯	Tong、; Tong、	Táng ; Tāng
Tsang	曾	Jang、	Zēng
Tse	謝	Je—	Xiè
Tung	董	Dung/	Dǒng
Wat	屈	Wat—	Qū
Wong	黃、王	Wong、	Huáng ; Wáng
Wu	胡	Woo、	Hú
Yau	游	Yau、	Yóu
Yeung	楊	Yeung、	Yáng
Yim	嚴	Yeem、	Yán
Yip	葉	Yeep—	Yè
Yiu	姚	Yu、	Yáo
Yu	余	Yü、	Yú
Yuen	阮、袁	Yün/ ; Yün、	Ruǎn ; Yuán
Yung	容、翁	Yung、; Yung、	Róng ; Wēng

Some Chinese Restaurants

Chiuchow City Restaurant	潮州城酒樓	Chyuˋ jauˋ Singˎ Jau´ lauˎ
Chiuchow Garden Restaurant	潮江春川菜館	Chyuˋ gongˋ Cheunˋ Chünˋ Choi- Gwoon´
City Hall Chinese Restaurant	大會堂酒樓	Daay_ wooyˋ tongˎ Jau´ lauˎ
East Ocean Seafood Restaurant	東海海鮮酒家	Dungˋ hoi´ Hoi´ seen- Jau´ gaaˋ
Guangzhou Garden Restaurant	粵江春	Yüt_ Gongˋ Cheunˋ
Hopewell City Restaurant	合和城酒樓	Hap_ worˋ singˎ Jau´ lauˎ
Hsin Kuang Restaurant	新光酒樓	Sanˋ Gwong- Jau´ lauˎ
Jade Garden Chinese Restaurant	翠園酒樓	Cheuy- Yün´ Jau´ lauˎ
Jumbo Floating Restaurant	珍寶海鮮舫	Janˋ bou´ Hoi´ seen- Fongˋ
Luk Yu Tea House	陸羽茶樓	Luk_ Yü´ Chaaˎ lauˎ
Ocean Palace Restaurant & Night Club	海洋皇宮大酒樓	Hoi´ yeungˋ Wongˋ gungˋ Daay_ Jau´ lauˎ
Peking Restaurant	北京樓	Bak- gingˋ Lauˎ
Pine & Bamboo Restaurant	松竹樓	Chungˎ Juk- Lauˎ
Round Dragon Chinese Restaurant	團龍閣	Tuen_ lungˋ Gok-
Senenade Chinese Restaurant	映月樓	Ying´ yüt_ Lauˎ
Shanghai Garden Restaurant	滬江春	Woo- gongˋ Cheunˋ
Shanghai Lao Ching Hing Restaurant	上海老正興菜館	Seungˎ hoi´ Lou´ jing- hingˋ Choi- Gwoon´
Sichuan Garden Restaurant	錦江春川菜館	Gam´ gongˋ Cheunˋ Chünˋ Choi- Gwoon´

Snow Garden Restaurant	雪園	Süt-	Yün´				
Tai Pak Floating Restaurant	太白海鮮舫	Taay-	baak_	Hoi´	seen¯	Fong´	
Tai Woo Restaurant	太湖海鮮城酒樓	Taay-	Woo\	Hoi´	seen¯	Sing\	Jau´ lau\
Treasure Restaurant	敦煌酒樓	Deun-	wong\	Jau´	lau\		
Tsui Hang Village Restaurant	翠亨邨茶寮	Cheuy-	hang\	Chün\	Chaa\	lyu\	
Windsor Palace Restaurant	溫莎皇宮酒樓	Wan\	saa\	Wong\	gung\	Jau´ lau\	
Winton Restaurant	運通泰酒樓	Wan_	tung\	taay-	Jau´	lau\	
Yat Tung Heen	逸東軒	Yat_	dung\	Heen¯			
Yuet Heung Restaurant	悅香飯店	Yüt-	heung\	Faan_	deem-		
Yung Kee Restaurant	鏞記酒家	Yung\	Gei-	Jau´	gaa\		